Care of Converts

With *Learning to Live* and Leader's Guide

Care of Converts

A Comprehensive Training Tool for Discipling New Believers

– Keith M. Bailey –

Christian Publications

CAMP HILL, PENNSYLVANIA

Christian Publications, Inc.
3825 Hartzdale Drive, Camp Hill, PA 17011

Faithful, biblical publishing since 1883

ISBN: 0-87509-707-3

© 1997 by Christian Publications, Inc.

Contents

Care of Converts

Care of Converts Leader's Guide

Appendix: Learning to Live

Care of Converts offers help in the disciple-making process. It seeks to help you and your church fulfill Paul's charge to Timothy: "And the things you have heard me say in the presence of many witnesses entrust to reliable men who will also be qualified to teach others" (2 Timothy 2:2). This discipling package is directed to two types of leaders:

1. The "Timothy" type of leader, who is training a group of "reliable men";

2. The "reliable men," the disciplers themselves, who are charged with the care of one or more new believers.

For the "Timothy"

The Leader's Guide section is written with you in mind.

There are a variety of ways this material can be used to train disciplers. For example, each chapter can be one lesson in an intensive, six-week training session; the Leader's Guide is structured around that format. But the material is very flexible, and many other formats are possible. You may wish to hold an introductory meeting before the six intensive sessions, in which copies of this book would be handed out to each participant and "ground rules" for the training would be laid down. You may also want to hold a wrap-up meeting to review the course and encourage the disciplers in their ministry.

Another possible format is to spend two sessions on each chapter. With an introductory or wrap-up session added, this could work well as a quarterly Sunday school class.

While group study has its advantages, the material can also be adapted to one-on-one training.

For the "Reliable Men"

While the main section of the book is written specifically for you, do not be shy about looking at the Leader's Guide, especially the discussion questions. If you have had a chance to think through the questions before the session, it can make for deeper, more lively class discussion.

If you are reading this book on your own, the discussion questions and activities in the Leader's Guide can help stimulate your thinking on the material. You may also find it helpful to review the material with your pastor or other spiritual leader to whom you can keep yourself accountable and with whom you can discuss the things you are learning.

The full text of *Learning to Live*, a new believer's Bible study, is included as an appendix. Part of your training can be to familiarize yourself with the Bible study and its related Scriptures (see "How to Use *Learning to Live*" on page 135). Separate copies of *Learning to Live* for new believers/ disciples are available from your local Christian bookstore or by calling Christian Publications at 1-800-233-4443.

Introduction

When they had finished eating, Jesus said to Simon Peter, "Simon son of John, do you truly love me more than these?"

"Yes, Lord," he said, "you know that I love you."

Jesus said, "Feed my lambs."

Again Jesus said, "Simon son of John, do you truly love me?"

He answered, "Yes, Lord, you know that I love you."

Jesus said, "Take care of my sheep."

The third time he said to him, "Simon son of John, do you love me?"

Peter was hurt because Jesus asked him the third time, "Do you love me?" He said, "Lord, you know all things; you know that I love you."

Jesus said, "Feed my sheep." (John 21:15-17)

The setting in which this moving dialogue took place was an early morning meeting of the disciples with Jesus on the shore of Galilee. The disciples had been fishing during the night and had received nothing for their efforts. Before daybreak a voice greeted them from the shore and instructed them to cast their net on the right side of the boat. Instantly the net filled with fish. The Stranger on the shore made Himself known to the disciples by this miraculous catch of fish. He was the risen Christ and He invited the astonished fishermen to join Him for breakfast.

After they had eaten, Jesus began a conversation with Peter. He must have sensed the deep remorse of the apostle at the thought of his denials of Jesus during the Savior's trial. The exchange between Christ and Peter found in these verses discloses some rich spiritual insight, but the passage also speaks to some practical issues. The three imperatives Christ gave the repentant Peter take in the whole spectrum of pastoral ministry. Jesus lovingly turns Peter's attention to the work he is destined to carry on in the future.

There is a progression in this series of directives. Jesus wanted Peter to understand that the whole family of God, both the lambs and the mature sheep, needs pastoral care. The starting point of all pastoral care is the feeding of the lambs. If lambs do not grow, there will be no sheep to tend.

This conversation had special meaning for Peter. Only days before he had fled from the Shepherd in His hour of trial. Peter was still suffering remorse and embarrassment over his failure. He was a lamb weak and vulnerable. Now the Shepherd of Love was tenderly ministering to him. Jesus fed this straying lamb with corrective truth.

The pastoral care demonstrated on that occasion by the Great Shepherd of the sheep sets an eternal pattern for the care of the people of God.

The lambs should be given priority in the ministry of shepherding. A Palestinian shepherd fed his flock by guiding them into green pastures and beside still waters. *Feed* refers to the shepherd's responsibility to find nourishment for the flock, a narrower meaning than *shepherd*.

In the second command Jesus said, "*Take care* of my sheep." The Greek word translated *Take care* applies to the whole ministry of pastoral care. To *shepherd* is to give lambs the tender, personal care they need in their infancy, gently leading and guiding them in every facet of their lives. No responsible shepherd would overlook the importance of nursing the lambs until their wobbly legs have strength to walk.

Jesus was using figurative language to describe the discipleship process when He said to Peter, "Feed My lambs." Total pastoral care includes the discipleship of new believers. A well-discipled lamb will become a well-disciplined sheep.

The contemporary concept of pastoral care is desperately weak in discipleship. That may be attributed at least in part to the erroneous notion that only the pastor can be involved in pastoral care. No pastor can care for so many people and do it well. Other leadership must be recruited and trained to assist in the pastoral care of the flock. This procedure is especially necessary for tending the lambs. New Christians need personal discipleship care. Lay people need to join hands with the pastor in giving this care.

The church needs first to develop a total church plan for follow-up ministries. Lay leaders should be trained to help in personal discipleship and in the various programs of corporate discipleship designed to integrate the new believer into the life of the total church.

Training a work force to disciple new Christians is as important as training a work force to evangelize. The discipler conserves the fruit of the evangelist. They complement one another in the process which makes converts complete in Christ.

This manual contains six lessons which address the need for discipleship, the methods of discipleship and the extent of discipleship. These chapters have been written with both the church's pastoral staff and lay leadership in mind.

Chapter 1

Dropouts or Disciples?

The record of evangelism in North America over the past thirty years shows a serious loss when the number of converts are compared with the number of people received into the fellowship of the church. Growth has been measured in terms of converts and that is not the best measure of success in evangelism. The most reliable measure of growth is the number of disciples added to the church. A disciple is a convert who is established in the Christian life and is functioning in the church. The convert who is not discipled will probably falter and eventually drop out of the spiritual race.

The annual reports of local churches provide some interesting case studies of this problem. Some congregations report a number of converts annually but over a ten-year period show little, if any, significant growth. In some cases, the number of active members actually became smaller. What do such churches do with new converts?

Consider the example of a church with an average attendance of 100 people on Sunday morning. The congregation is about forty years old. At least once a year the congregation has a series of evangelistic meetings. A summer vacation Bible school is conducted for children. Some visitation evangelism is carried on. The aggregate number of converts from these various outreach programs in a given year averages thirty-five. An accumulative increase at this rate for a ten-year period would be 350 new Christians. It is startling to discover that after ten years the membership of the church shows no significant increase and the attendance remains much as it was at the beginning—there has actually been no growth.

What became of those converts? The loss of 350 people who confessed Jesus Christ is very, very tragic. Had that congregation learned and applied some simple principles of follow-up they could have conserved most of the fruit for that period of time. Rather than being at the same static membership figure they could now be a congregation in excess of 400 with a much larger work force available to reach their community for Christ and to assist the whole church in its common goal of evangelizing the world.

What did they do wrong? They failed to take names and addresses so that contacts could be made with people who professed in their meetings in the church or in contacts outside the church. One of the elders thought that it wasn't spiritual to keep such records.

This church had failed to take water baptism seriously. New converts were not urged to follow the Lord in baptism. Over the ten-year period there was an average of less than one baptism per year. Only about two percent of those who had received the Lord as Savior were baptized.

The number of people brought into the church fellowship was more startling. After ten years the membership had increased by only ten. We cannot complete the story of this church without noticing that during this same time period they suffered the loss of eighty-five percent of the young people from the families of their congregation.

If this congregation were an isolated case, one might not be so alarmed. But if you look at the average evangelical church in North America, you will discover that far too many churches maintain the attitude reflected by this example. New methods of evangelism and outreach will not cure the problem we have just described. That church proved it had ability to reach new people for Christ. It failed at the point of discipling those converts so that they would become a vital part of Christ's church.

Dr. C.E. Autrey of the Southern Baptist Convention says of our day: "The churches of the twentieth century have done a far better job of evangelizing than they have of nurturing."[1] With the widespread renewal of evangelism it is imperative that both lay and pastoral leadership give serious consideration to the implications of discipleship. Is our goal just to count converts or is our goal like that of the apostle Paul—to present every man perfect in Christ?

Pastors and lay leaders will probably meet resistance when they begin to correct the errors that have fostered such great losses to the church of Jesus Christ. Ill-founded traditions without biblical base have led many Christians astray at this point. Churches have fostered the foolish notion that new converts should be left to themselves until they have proved their spiritual strength and power. If perchance they survive, the church leadership will then approach them about membership and involvement in the church. This practice is unbiblical. It is totally unlike the primitive church described in the book of Acts.

The remarkable growth of the churches of the first century can be largely attributed to their ability to conserve the results of evangelistic outreach. To sustain such growth, the modern church needs to go back to the biblical follow-up practices of the early church to disciple every new convert.

In a very succinct statement, Dr. C.E. Autrey has captured the essence of discipleship from a theological point of view:

> The new converts must be led to understand their experience with Christ. They must be taught the meaning of love and of Christian living. They must be taught biblical methods and how to use them with proper motivation. Never let the church take these things for granted. Bib-

*lical methods are theologically unsound if not
properly motivated. Teach them that they were
redeemed to witness and that they are prepared
only if they worship, study the Bible, pray and
are endued with the Holy Spirit.* [2]

There are certain telltale signs of the neglect of
new converts in evangelical churches. One of the
most obvious is the large number of people that confess Christ but will not give allegiance to any
church. They float on the sea of religious activity
with no sense of direction. They hasten from sacred
concert to sacred concert, from Bible conference to
Bible conference, from seminar to seminar, from
movement to movement, preoccupied with hero-
image leadership. These unattached Christians are
easy prey to certain types of spectacular leadership.
They are tasters of sermons more often than they
are doers of the Word. If everything does not contribute to their self-centered view of the church,
they move on to hear the latest religious star in the
vain hope that they have at last found the answer.
Well-discipled believers would not fall into that kind
of hopeless syndrome.

Another sign that indicates a need for discipleship is the many believers that do not grow up:
they remain babes in Christ and require constant
care. They are problem-centered, wanting a
church ministry that provides spiritual props. The
pastoral staff counsels many Christians who, in
the light of Scripture, should now be equipped to
counsel others.

So much of the church's manpower and resources is absorbed in maintenance of the church
family that evangelistic outreach takes a minor
role in the mission of the church if it has any role
at all.

As believers are added to the fellowship, the
church's work force should be increasing. Out of
the whole body there should be an adequate number of people to minister to needs of the saints and
an adequate work force to minister to the community in evangelistic outreach. Most modern Christians never join either work force. They have
never been taught the divine plan for their lives as
disciples of the Lord Jesus Christ.

The writer to the Hebrews lamented this condition among the believers he addresses in that epistle.

> *In fact, though by this time you ought to be
> teachers, you need someone to teach you the ele-
> mentary truths of God's word all over again.
> You need milk, not solid food! Anyone who lives
> on milk, being still an infant, is not acquainted
> with the teaching about righteousness. But solid
> food is for the mature, who by constant use have
> trained themselves to distinguish good from evil.
> (Hebrews 5:12-14)*

The condition of prolonged spiritual infancy is,
in most cases, the result of poor discipleship or of
no discipleship at all. Converts are no more able to
care for themselves than babies are able to care for

themselves. Neglect of new converts at this stage tends to make them spiritual dropouts or it locks them into permanent babyhood. Converts who were destined to be stalwart servants of Christ and His church remain infants in need of perpetual care.

The best preventative for the recurrence of this spiritual tragedy is a good follow-up ministry in the local church. It must be a follow-up approach that produces disciples.

There are basic principles to be observed in building a church follow-up program. Both pastoral and lay leaders should be involved in building and carrying out the ministry of discipling those who profess faith in Christ.

Begin with a study of the facts about your own congregation. The following statistics are vital to this study:

1. The number of active members

2. The number of adherents

3. The average attendance at the regular services of the church

4. The number of converts

5. The number of baptisms

6. The number of new members

The new-member category should be divided to reflect those new members by profession of faith and transfers from other congregations who are already Christians. This device will show the growth by conversion as compared with the growth by transfer. It would be helpful to prepare a line graph of these statistics showing either the increase or decrease in each category. The percentage of increase per year and the cumulative percentages should also be worked out.

Such a study will help local church leadership to bring into focus the areas of weakness in their program. Steps can be taken to develop a total church program of discipleship.

The author conducted a seminar on evangelism in a church that had just finished a series of evangelistic meetings. A total of nineteen adults had professed Christ as Savior in the course of the ten-day meetings. The elders had selected gospel portions and some tracts for converts to take home after they had been counseled at the altar of prayer. Beyond this point there had been no serious consideration of a plan for discipleship for these new Christians. Upon questioning the elders about this, it was learned that they assumed the pastor would care for these new believers. It was pointed out to them that should the pastor assume this task every entire work week for the next three months, he would be consumed in basic discipleship of these new Christians. He would have no time to prepare sermons, to visit the sick, to counsel the troubled of the congregation or to tend to necessary administrative responsibilities in the life of the church.

For the first time Sunday school teachers, elders, deacons and deaconesses in that congregation became aware of the fact that the care of new converts is more than a pastoral function. It is a total church function, and one they are to be involved in. The discovery of the importance of lay involvement in follow-up was a turning point in the life of that church.

Every truly successful evangelistic church has learned this secret and has developed within its leadership many lay people capable of the work of discipleship.

Leadership training for follow-up is not designed just for pastors. It should include elders, deacons, Sunday school workers and teachers, workers with boys and girls in the clubs, youth workers in the church and all who have any serious concern in the winning of souls to Jesus Christ and the eternal welfare of those souls.

Not a day should be lost in building a nucleus of well-informed follow-up workers.

To fail in follow-up in making disciples is to risk the converts becoming spiritual drones in the church or becoming spiritual dropouts.

Endnotes

1. C.E. Autrey, *The Theology of Evangelism* (Nashville, TN: Broadman Press, 1966).

2. Ibid., p. 57.

Chapter 2

What Is a Disciple?

The Church has been mandated by her risen Lord to make disciples. The mission of the Church is not just to make converts but to make disciples of the converts.

The term *convert* means one who professes Christ as Savior and shows a change in the direction of his or her life.

Converts are those who have turned from sin to follow Christ. To follow Jesus Christ is to be a disciple. There should, therefore, be no lag between being a convert and becoming a disciple. The care of a convert begins as soon as faith in Christ is professed. Discipleship cares and nurtures new disciples until they are mature, functioning members of the local church.

Before tracing the steps in the discipleship process the meaning of discipleship must be clear. *Disciple* is a term peculiar to the four Gospels and the book of Acts. The Greek word *mathetes* is found 250 times in those five books of the New

Testament. *Follower* seems to be a synonym for *disciple* but it is found only twice outside of the Gospels and Acts. The term *disciple* can also be found in the sub-apostolic literature of the church and carries the same meaning as in the canonical Scriptures.

The term *disciple* had a secular meaning in the culture of Jesus' day. It spoke of the student-teacher relationship. Disciples were common in the academic world and in the cultic religions of the day; they had been sitting at the feet of Greek and Roman philosophers for centuries before Christ. The association of the master-teacher with the disciple-student was much more than a class-room situation. The disciple lived with his teacher and followed his way of life as well as his system of dogma.

The pagan religious world knew of a similar relationship. The new devotees of the mystic cults were initiated and prepared for the cultic worship and life by a discipleship process. It would appear that wherever Christians went in the first century the idea of discipleship was known.

Discipleship was not unknown to Jewish culture. John the Baptist, the forerunner of Jesus, had disciples, some of whom eventually became disciples of Christ. Pharisees and other Jewish sects had disciples as well. The pupil-teacher relationship was the form of discipleship familiar to the Jewish community.

A disciple then is a pupil. He is a learner. He has come under the influence of a teacher for whom he has great admiration, one he seeks to emulate both in precept and practice. To be a true disciple of Christ one must learn the truth of the gospel and the walk of the Christian. He must keep learning with the view of becoming a teacher.

A disciple is an adherent. He or she gives loyal support to Christ and to His cause and is not ashamed to be identified openly with the Lord Jesus Christ. Like Christ's disciples in the gospel record, modern disciples must take their stand with Christ before the people. Discipleship means clinging to Christ no matter what the situation.

There is a sense in which every true follower of Christ is an apprentice. The skills of Christian living and service must be acquired under the careful tutorage of a good teacher. The master workman must begin as an apprentice. He is taught the precepts of the craft and trained in applying them. The discipleship process keeps in view the goal of producing a workman sanctified and ready for the Master's use.

A familiar synonym for disciple is *follower*, one who walks behind Jesus one step at a time, resisting all temptations designed to divert him from Christ's way. The footsteps of Jesus set the disciple's pace and direction in life. The disciple turns from all other paths to follow Christ with complete devotion. Discipleship begins with the first step but must continue step by step in the path of righteousness.

The disciple follows the master-teacher because he sees him possessing superior knowledge. In a true disciple-to-teacher relationship the disciple is being formed in the image of his teacher. Basically, discipleship is following the greatest of master-teachers, the Lord Jesus Christ Himself. But discipleship is also following another experienced and seasoned disciple of Christ who can guide, guard and nurture the new disciple in his crucial first days of spiritual growth.

The term *disciple* as used by Jesus and the apostles meant a Christian. The disciples were first called Christians at Antioch (Acts 11:26). There were other designations for Christian believers. Christ spoke of them as children, believers, friends and brothers. The word *disciple* is a special designation which has reference to certain aspects of the believer's life. It describes the convert as a pupil being readied for a more mature life and work.

Discipleship is the process that brings a new believer to maturity. It's the "boot camp" training period and therefore critical to the future of the believer. This progression helps a new believer work his way through a number of basic issues in the Christian life.

Jesus taught six issues that confront all who would be His disciples. He gave no room for exceptions. All who follow Christ must follow this pathway. The credibility of one's walk as a disciple is determined by one's reaction to these issues. The first fundamental issue of Christian discipleship is found in John's Gospel:

> *To the Jews who had believed him, Jesus said,*
> *"If you hold to my teaching, you are really my*
> *disciples. Then you will know the truth, and the*
> *truth will set you free." (John 8:31-32)*

The disciple, says Jesus, embraces the truth and finds in it liberating power. Knowing the truth is the prerequisite to spiritual freedom. Jesus said that His Word is the truth. The truth has been recorded in the inspired Scriptures. Freedom from sin and the shackles of the old life is found in knowing that truth.

The distorted and futile thinking of the sinner must be forever forsaken. A new mind furnished with truth becomes the control center for a true disciple of Christ. He has turned from darkness to light. The man or woman who clings to darkness can make no claim to discipleship.

The second identifying mark of a disciple is that he bears fruit. Jesus said,

> *If you remain in me and my words remain in*
> *you, ask whatever you wish, and it will be given*
> *you. This is to my Father's glory, that you bear*
> *much fruit, showing yourselves to be my disci-*
> *ples. (John 15:7-8)*

The reality of discipleship is tested by the fruit the believer bears. When there is no fruit there is no substantial evidence of spiritual life. Fruit-bearing is inherent in the life implanted in the heart by one's relationship to Christ. His very own life flows into His follower to produce the spiritual qualities that please Him. If the believer, by disobedience, resistance or ignorance, resists that life flow, the believer becomes nonproductive.

A third test of discipleship found in the teachings of Christ requires that the interest of Christ be first in the life of a disciple.

> *If anyone comes to me and does not hate his father and mother, his wife and children, his brothers and sisters—yes, even his own life—he cannot be my disciple.* (Luke 14:26)

No more shocking words than these ever came from the Savior's lips. How can this statement be reconciled with the rest of the New Testament which teaches the family responsibilities incumbent upon a Christian? The verb *hate* is the key to interpreting this passage. John is saying that your love for those dearest to you will seem like hate when compared with your love for Him. He is to be first and foremost in the affections of a disciple.

The practical effect of this truth becomes evident when moral and spiritual choices must be made by the believer. A disciple will choose to please Christ at the expense of displeasing some or all of his family. The believer's love for Christ is to be supreme.

The fourth badge of discipleship given by Christ is cross-bearing.

Then he said to them all: "If anyone would come after me, he must deny himself and take up his cross daily and follow me. (Luke 9:23)

And anyone who does not carry his cross and follow me cannot be my disciple. (Luke 14:27)

The high-water mark of the plan of redemption is the atonement. The death of Jesus Christ on the cross effected a complete and perfect atonement for all who believe. Believers not only trust Christ's death on that old rugged cross to bring about forgiveness, reconciliation and cleansing, but by faith they must accept the curse of the cross upon the self-life and the power of indwelling sin. It is customary to associate this concept with deeper life teaching, and it is that, but unfortunately believers often are not introduced to this truth until they are well along in their Christian life. Jesus made cross-bearing an issue of initial discipleship. Death to self is a foundational truth disciples need to understand from the beginning of their new life in Christ. As they grow, their understanding of self-denial will be greater, but it is a condition of discipleship from the start.

Those who have the responsibility of instructing new disciples either individually or in a group do well to explain the way of the cross and urge every disciple to walk in it.

A fifth mark of discipleship is found in Luke 14, where Jesus said,

*"In the same way, any of you who does not give
up everything he has cannot be my disciple."*
(Luke 14:33)

The way of discipleship is costly. No one
should enter it without considering fully the implications of such a commitment. The disciples of
Jesus Christ must be willing to turn over all their
earthly possessions to Christ and to follow Him
no matter what the cost. Such a rugged calling can
be met only by a life of faith. The true follower of
Jesus does not hesitate to walk the road of hard-
ship or even poverty for the Master's sake. He
knows by faith that Christ will meet his need. The
footstep followers of Jesus Christ find the Calvary
road a royal highway to heavenly riches that are
eternal.

The sixth, supreme identifying mark of a disciple of Jesus Christ is found in John 13. On that
wonderful night in the upper room while Jesus
and His disciples were at the supper table the Savior gave a great object lesson in spiritual truth by
washing the disciples' feet. Jesus concluded the
discourse on the meaning of that event with a new
commandment:

*A new command I give you: Love one another.
As I have loved you, so you must love one another. By this all men will know that you are
my disciples, if you love one another.* (John
13:34-35).

While following Christ is a very personal way of life, it is also a community way of life. One cannot be a disciple in isolation from the church of Christ. The divine standard requires love for our brothers and sisters. It is not possible to sincerely love Christ and not love His people. Jesus points out the fact that to the populous the credibility of any claim to being a disciple of Jesus rests on a visible demonstration of love within the Christian community. People in the world often become disillusioned with Christianity because of the absence of love among believers. Apostolic Christianity made a deep impact on the whole world in its day. Pagans, as they observed the lives of the early Christians, exclaimed, "Behold how they love one another." Open, gracious manifestation of divine love is the only sign of discipleship unbelievers can read.

The process of discipleship does not make one a believer, but it matures the work of grace begun in conversion. Oswald Chambers, renowned British devotional writer, says;

> *Salvation and discipleship are not one and the same. Whenever our Lord speaks of discipleship He prefaces what He has to say with an "if." "If any man come after me." Discipleship is based on devotion to Jesus Christ, not on adherence to a doctrine.*[1]

It is therefore obvious that disciples are not made by teaching alone. Unless the indoctrination awakens a deep devotion to Christ the follow-up procedure will fail. The Church is not left to design its own standard for measuring disciples. The teachings of Jesus on this subject remain mandatory. The time has come for the Church to humbly return to the Savior's standard and method of making disciples.

Everything Jesus had to say about being a disciple called for discipline. To walk in the path He prescribes requires a high level of self-control. In a day of self-indulgence and easy living, self-discipline is not popular. The greatest single task in discipling modern converts is to make them see the necessity of discipline. Follow-up programs which fail to confront the new Christian with the conditions of discipleship laid down by Jesus fall short of the mark. They may produce devoted followers of a cause but not disciples in the sense of the New Testament.

Dr. V. Raymond Edman, late president of Wheaton College, in a chapel message on discipline, said:

> *Discipleship means discipline! The disciple is that one who has been taught or trained by the Master, who has come with his ignorance, superstition and sin to find learning, truth and forgiveness from the Savior. Without discipline we are not disciples, even though we profess His name and pass for a follower of the lowly Nazarene. In an undisciplined age when liberty and license have replaced law and loyalty, there is*

greater need than ever before that we be disciplined to be His disciples.[2]

The disciplines of discipleship build character. They bring into focus the spiritual issues that must be faced by those who would follow Christ. The popular lecturer and Bible teacher, William Sanford Lasor, defines a disciple as one who comes under the discipline of another.[3]

The true disciple must have a teachable spirit. He dwells with his teacher, for much of the discipline of discipleship is instruction by concept and example. The new convert must be taught to manifest devotion, dedication, loyalty, holiness, maturity and integrity by the Master's plan for making disciples. The Scriptures offer no alternatives to discipleship. The absence of this process in the operation of the average evangelical church is the direct cause of so much of our spiritual poverty. Failure to make disciples retards the growth of the church and delays the evangelization of the world.

Endnotes

1. Oswald Chambers, *If Thou Wilt Be Perfect* (London, Simpkin Marshall Ltd., 1939.), pp. 104-105.

2. V. Raymond Edman, *The Disciplines of Life* (Chicago, IL: Van Kampen Press.), p. 93.

3. William S. Lasor, *Men Who Knew Christ* (Glendale, CA: Regal Books 1971), p. 41.

Chapter 3

Biblical Models of Discipleship

The New Testament, in addition to giving a mandate for follow-up ministry, gives some examples of success when it is implemented. The inspired Scriptures provide for the guidance of Christians in every generation a cross section of the follow-up ministry in the apostolic church. These examples are rich in insights for the pastors and lay leaders who are called upon to care for new believers.

Every congregation needs a corps of workers for follow-up. Selecting the right people for this work is critical to its success. God equips some believers with just the right combination of qualities for helping new believers get a good start in the Christian life. Part of the management of any work force is to place people where they are best fitted to work. The oversight of the church requires leadership to assign work on this same principle. The pastor and elders should give thought

to men and women whose qualities of temperament and of spiritual maturity fit them for follow-
up.

Three Model Disciplers

Let us consider three outstanding models of discipleship ministry from the New Testament. Each
of them had particular skill in caring for lambs.

Barnabas

The first study is on Barnabas, known among
his fellow-workers as the "son of encouragement."
Barnabas had great financial resources, but upon
becoming a committed believer he sold his land
holdings and gave the profit to the church. (See
Acts 4:36-37.) Self-sacrifice characterized the lifestyle of this first-century Christian. His love and
devotion to Christ made it easy for him to give his
all to the Lord.

Early in his ministry Barnabas learned the importance of trusting a new Christian. It ought not
to be true but believers more mature in the faith
are often cautious with and suspicious of new believers, expecting them to be as mature as Christians who have been walking with the Lord for
many years.

When Saul of Tarsus received Christ the
Church was alarmed. Many thought he only
feigned faith in Christ as part of a plot to imprison
more Christians. Had it not been for two discern-
ing Christians who understood Paul and helped
him, he would have been hard put to effectively

minister to the Church. Barnabas, being sensitive to Paul's situation, went out of his way to encourage this new believer and to help him relate to the Church and its leaders.

Modern churches are no different than the Jerusalem congregation with regard to this problem. Mature believers expect new converts to prove themselves. That terminology sounds pious but it really means that they do not trust new believers. Such an attitude defeats the cause of evangelism. It brings discouragement and disillusionment to the recently saved and makes more difficult their transition from the old life to the new. Every newborn soul needs a Barnabas who really understands, someone to soften the transition process. Barnabas, unwilling to accept the prevailing attitude regarding Paul, sought Paul out and encouraged him.

> But Barnabas took him and brought him to the apostles. He told them how Saul on his journey had seen the Lord and that the Lord had spoken to him, and how in Damascus he had preached fearlessly in the name of Jesus. (Acts 9:27)

Barnabas was willing to put his own spiritual reputation on the line for Paul's sake. Such a course of action paid rich dividends in the end. Paul enjoyed a long and useful missionary career in the spread of the gospel among the Gentiles. It is not difficult to imagine what could have happened to Paul had there been no Barnabas to disciple him.

By the time the gospel had spread to Antioch Barnabas already had a reputation in the church as being gifted in dealing with new believers. The church in Jerusalem heard of the moving of the Spirit in Antioch that came as a result of Philip's preaching. The leadership at Jerusalem realized the need for establishing these new Christians and immediately dispatched Barnabas for the task.

> Some of them, however, men from Cyprus and Cyrene, went to Antioch and began to speak to Greeks also, telling them the good news about the Lord Jesus. The Lord's hand was with them, and a great number of people believed and turned to the Lord.
>
> News of this reached the ears of the church at Jerusalem, and they sent Barnabas to Antioch. When he arrived and saw the evidence of the grace of God, he was glad and encouraged them all to remain true to the Lord with all their hearts. He was a good man, full of the Holy Spirit and faith, and a great number of people were brought to the Lord.
>
> Then Barnabas went to Tarsus to look for Saul, and when he found him, he brought him to Antioch. So for a whole year Barnabas and Saul met with the church and taught great numbers of people. The disciples were called Christians first at Antioch. (Acts 11:20-26)

Barnabas sensed that the evangelistic work being done in Antioch was real and set about at once to establish the new believers. Barnabas used at least five different means in the follow-up of the revival at Antioch.

His first reaction to this work of God was to rejoice. Positive joy is the best atmosphere for initial follow-up. Barnabas praised God for the work He had accomplished in the lives of the converts. He openly showed his joy to their encouragement.

The second step in Barnabas' program for follow-up was encouragement. This gentle-spirited man had a way of encouraging right decisions that would strengthen the walk of the convert. His exhortations were firm. Being a realist, he knew the trials and testings to which those new Christians were exposed. By word and action Barnabas urged them to stand true to the Lord. He did not adopt a hands-off policy to see how they would turn out. Barnabas knew that the converts needed his constant exhortation to help them cope with the struggles of the new life.

One overriding contribution of Barnabas to the discipleship process was his untarnished example. He practiced the kind of walk he advocated the new believer to adopt. Barnabas displayed the Spirit-filled life. His walk was consistent. His character was credible. His faith was conquering. The new Christian could see in the example of Barnabas that the Christian walk would endure. The quality of life Barnabas demonstrated was a key factor in establishing a multitude of new believers at Antioch.

The program Barnabas had gotten from the Lord called for instruction. Example, encouragement and exhortation are not going to do the work of establishing believers unless they are attended by teaching. Christianity is an encounter with Christ that produces reality in experience. But it is also a system of truth to be understood. Without sound doctrine no program of follow-up will work.

The concern Barnabas had to adequately teach these new converts impelled him to seek help with this ministry. He remembered his former disciple, Paul, and recruited him as his co-worker. With Paul as his helper Barnabas launched a year-long program of intense teaching. The fact that it took a year to complete the teaching would indicate that Barnabas did a thorough job.

Contemporary pastors and lay leaders should learn from the program of Barnabas. Teaching of a poor quality and in a limited amount starts the converts on their way woefully unprepared for the work, the walk and the warfare of the Christian life. A complete and basic doctrinal system should be given all who come to Christ.

Paul was deeply impressed by his experience with Barnabas at Antioch. Throughout his ministry he gave major attention to teaching his converts. By classes, by person-to-person contact and by letters Paul taught newborn believers the system of objective truth they needed to survive spiritually. Modern evangelical churches need to examine afresh the apostle's procedure. Classes for new converts ought to be an ongoing part of every church program.

The follow-up practice of Barnabas produced quality in the church at Antioch. The lives of the believers of this new church made such an impression on that pagan city that they were nicknamed "Christians," literally meaning "little Christs." Well-established believers should reflect the Christ-life even to the unconverted.

The responsibility of the Church is to see that every true convert gets a good start. To do any less than that is to see most of the converts fall away. Those who do survive often live faltering lives and are many years coming to any level of maturity. What Barnabas learned from the Holy Spirit about conserving the results holds good today. Personal concern, a good example, gentle exhortation and sound teaching transform converts into functioning Christians.

Ananias

Ananias, another model discipler, had strong influence on Paul at the beginning of his Christian life. He was a layman who lived in the city of Damascus. One day while Ananias was at prayer the Lord spoke to him:

> In Damascus there was a disciple named Ananias. The Lord called to him in a vision, "Ananias!"

> *"Yes, Lord," he answered.*
> *The Lord told him, "Go to the house of Judas*
> *on Straight Street and ask for a man from Tar-*
> *sus named Saul, for he is praying.* (Acts 9:10-
> 11)

Ananias' heart was struck with terror at the name of Saul, the man who had a reputation as the principal leader of the persecution against Christians. This militant persecutor, Saul of Tarsus, had been converted, and the Lord had selected Ananias to disciple him. This was an important assignment, for Paul was destined to become the leading gospel preacher of his time. It is interesting that the Lord chose a layman to deal with him rather than one of the apostles. Evidently Ananias was both capable and well prepared for this ministry.

The Scripture simply designates Ananias as a disciple. Ananias was very sensitive to the guidance of the Holy Spirit. The Spirit directed him to Paul who, though only a Christian for three days, was earnestly seeking God in prayer. Ananias instructed Paul and gave immediate attention to his needs. It is amazing in the light of modern practice that Ananias brought Paul to the Spirit-filled life only three days after his conversion. He also brought Paul to water baptism. No doubt the Spirit-led discipleship care Ananias gave Paul had an ongoing effect on his life. It would appear that Paul gave the same kind of care to his own converts.

Timothy

The third model of follow-up ministry in the New Testament is Timothy. Paul himself had discipled this promising young convert. Paul often thought of discipleship as a father-son relationship rather than that of a pupil-teacher. As young Timothy became firmly established he was entrusted with the care of other babes in Christ. Paul often assigned Timothy to follow-up the fruits of their missionary labors. While Paul moved to new fields of evangelism Timothy, the teacher, would stay to disciple the converts. Paul said to him:

> *You then, my son, be strong in the grace that is in Christ Jesus. And the things you have heard me say in the presence of many witnesses entrust to reliable men who will also be qualified to teach others.* (2 Timothy 2:1-2)

Follow-up ministry for Timothy was passing on to his converts what had been given him. He expected a level of spiritual growth in the converts whereby they would be able to teach others.

The Goal of Follow-up

The apostle Paul had a well-formulated objective for his follow-up ministry:

> *Now I rejoice in what was suffered for you, and I fill up in my flesh what is still lacking in regard to Christ's afflictions, for the sake of his*

body, which is the church. I have become its ser-
vant by the commission God gave me to present
to you the word of God in its fullness—the mys-
tery that has been kept hidden for ages and gen-
erations, but is now disclosed to the saints. To
them God has chosen to make known among the
Gentiles the glorious riches of this mystery,
which is Christ in you, the hope of glory.

We proclaim him, admonishing and teaching
everyone with all wisdom, so that we may pre-
sent everyone perfect in Christ. To this end I la-
bor, struggling with all his energy, which so
powerfully works in me.

I want you to know how much I am strug-
gling for you and for those at Laodicea, and for
all who have not met me personally. My purpose
is that they may be encouraged in heart and
united in love, so that they may have the full
riches of complete understanding, in order that
they may know the mystery of God, namely,
Christ, in whom are hidden all the treasures of
wisdom and knowledge. I tell you this so that no
one may deceive you by fine-sounding argu-
ments. For though I am absent from you in
body, I am present with you in spirit and delight
to see how orderly you are and how firm your
faith in Christ is. (Colossians 1:24-2:5)

Paul's objective was to "present everyone perfect in Christ" (Colossians 1:28). The task of evangelism is not finished until this goal has been
reached. Certainly Paul did not have in mind ab-

solute perfection when he said "perfect in Christ."
Rather he was thinking of the same truth he dis-
cusses in the fourth chapter of Ephesians when he
speaks of believers being brought into "the whole
measure of the fullness of Christ" (4:13).

The apostle Paul structured his ministry and
that of his co-workers to achieve the goal of presenting everyone perfect in Christ. Much of their
energy was put into the discipleship of their converts. Follow-up was so important in the thinking
of Paul that he labored at it with a great deal of energy.

He sought spiritual power to carry out this ministry. He said to the Christians in Colosse that he
had had a great struggle on their behalf. He had
labored mightily for them. Discipleship is hard
work, but it is very rewarding since the end product becomes a functioning, reproducing Christian,
one who is complete in Christ.

In Colossians 1:28, the apostle Paul gives his
own method of discipleship. Three key words describe his method: *Proclaim, admonish* and *teach*.

He Proclaimed

Proclaiming is preaching; preaching is setting
forth the propositional statements from God's revealed Word and urging their authority upon the
hearer. The modern Church should not forget the
importance of preaching in follow-up. Small
group discussions, good reading, one-on-one attention and concern will help the new Christian,
but over and above all of these he needs to hear

good, solid Bible preaching. On occasion the pastor ought to remember as he is preparing for the preaching of the Word of God that a part of preaching is to disciple converts. His sermons ought to inspire, excite and move the new child of God in the direction of full commitment to the Lord Jesus Christ.

He Admonished

Paul not only preached to new Christians, but he also admonished them. An admonition is often more personal and direct than preaching. It addresses itself to the practical problems of the Christian life, advising new believers as to how they should walk and how they should serve the Lord Jesus Christ, pointing out the flaws in their daily walk and showing them how to strengthen themselves in the Lord.

He Taught

The third term used by Paul is teaching or setting forth in a systematic manner the basic doctrines of the Bible. Every Christian needs a doctrinal education. It is sometimes popular to say that doctrine does not count. That statement is not biblical. Soundness of faith and strength of spiritual life and vitality for service are all related to proper doctrine. Most of the difficulties in the church are due to improper teaching with regard to doctrine. The new Christian ought to have exposure to sound teaching from the very inception of his spiritual life.

This raises the question, "What should the follow-up procedure produce in new Christians?" We have already determined that they should know and understand basic Christian doctrine. Secondly, they should know how to feed their own soul from the Word of God. They should have developed some skills in the study of the Scriptures. They should have learned how to pray and to exercise faith, how to cope with trials and the pressures of life by going to the Lord in prayer. They should also know how to witness— to speak to someone else about the claims of Christ. They should know the steps and the plan of salvation so well as to be able to instruct another. In other words, they should be personal soul winners.

The new Christian should have discovered those biblical principles by which to guide him in separation from the spirit of the world and the practices of the world so that his life has integrity. He should have learned how to relate to his family as a Christian. If he is the head of the household, his role in that position means that his Christian influence is very important and that he becomes the high priest of the Christian home. If the new Christian is a teenager or a child or the wife in the home, that new Christian should learn how to relate to the unconverted members of the household, to bear a testimony and to maintain a spiritual walk that will attract the unconverted. He should be consistently growing in the grace and knowledge of the Lord Jesus Christ. He should also know how to cope with persecution and with suffering so that his spiritual life is not seriously injured when difficulties come across his pathway.

Age Levels of Spiritual Growth

It is God's plan for a newborn Christian to grow up and become a spiritual adult. The New Testament delineates spiritual age groups. The apostle John speaks of little children, young men and fathers. Careful examination of this passage makes clear that John had in mind three different categories of Christians. The terms he uses have nothing to do with physical age, but rather relate to spiritual age. John too had a goal in his discipleship program, which was to make all the little children young men and then fathers. John says:

> *I write to you, dear children,*
>   *because your sins have been forgiven*
>   *on account of his name.*
> *I write to you, fathers,*
>   *because you have known him who*
>   *is from the beginning.*
> *I write to you, young men,*
>   *because you have overcome the evil*
>   *one.*
> *I write to you, dear children,*
>   *because you have known the Father.*
> *I write to you, fathers,*
>   *because you have known him who is*
>   *from the beginning.*

> *I write to you, young men,*
> *because you are strong,*
> *and the word of God lives in you,*
> *and you have overcome the evil one.*
> (1 John 2:12-14)

The newborn Christian knows God through Christ and a conscious witness of his sins forgiven, but the mature Christian, the complete Christian, has learned how to overcome. He has learned the Word of God and has it is abiding in him. And he has gained an experiential knowledge of Christ.

The Full Cycle of Evangelism

The New Testament teaches follow-up not only by the models of follow-up ministry it records but it also states the concept theologically. Follow-up is inherent in the Great Commission given by Christ to the Church.

> *Therefore go and make disciples of all nations,*
> *baptizing them in the name of the Father and of*
> *the Son and of the Holy Spirit, and teaching*
> *them to obey everything I have commanded you.*
> *And surely I am with you always, to the very*
> *end of the age.* (Matthew 28:19-20)

The full cycle of evangelism is described in this passage. To go is not enough. Those who go must disciple people for Christ. Those who make converts must baptize and teach them. North American-style evangelism too frequently stops at the

point of conversion. Christ did not stop with conversion and we dare not stop at that point either.
The Church must reform its practice so as to
carry out the whole of the mandate for evangelism
which Christ left us.

Chapter 4

Personal Discipleship

Among the methods of evangelistic outreach none are more productive than personal evangelism. Individual believers witness to unbelievers and bring those with a concern to a decision. Just as the personal approach was a key factor in their conversion such new believers are helped by personal discipleship. One person is assigned to care for and guide the new convert through the discipleship process.

A number of members should be chosen and trained to carry on personal discipleship. As a person is saved he or she is assigned to a mature Christian for initial spiritual nurture. The person responsible for discipling a new believer may be called a "fellowship-partner" and acts as a sponsor, friend, parent and teacher to the growing disciple.

People with gifts that will make them effective should be chosen for this ministry. They must have gentle and patient dispositions. The disciples should be steady, well-established Christians. Those who undertake this aspect of total church evangelism must be fully dedicated and filled with the Holy Spirit. They are asked to perform a difficult task which is not a public ministry and is therefore often unnoticed, even in the fellowship of the Church. But it pleases God and emulates Christ's own devotion to His disciples.

At the 1965 summer Keswick Convention held in Britain the Rev. E.J. Alexander brought a message on "Christian Growth, Maturity and Service." He addressed the matter of discipleship and those responsible for the work:

> We have in Christ by the Holy Spirit a new birth; and when we have a new birth, naturally we become babies. And the task of the people of God and the Church of God, when babes in Christ are to be found among them, is to care for them and nurture them and yearn over them and guard them and watch over them with all constant attention of a mother over her newborn child.
>
> This is a challenge to the Church of God in these days, and to us as individual Christians. It is one thing, you see, to be gladly willing to go out to attend meetings or to take some prominent public part within the Church of God; but there is a costliness about taking someone under your wing who is newborn, with all the awkwardness and weakness, and sheer stupidity at times of the

*newborn creature. I'm persuaded that there is a
ministry here which is costly and secret, but very
precious in the eyes of the Lord; the ministry of
the man or woman within the Church of God
who is ready to take newborns and to nurture
them into growth and maturity.* "[1]

Pastor Alexander has given a rather complete
job description of those who disciple and has
placed such a ministry in proper perspective. The
ministry to disciple newborn souls is a necessity.
To recruit and prepare such a work force is the responsibility of every church which seeks to win
the lost.

The first twelve weeks after conversion are
critical. Proper care during this period can mean
the difference between a spiritual dropout and a
growing Christian. In a large church if the pastor
must make all contacts with that new convert, he
may visit only once in twelve weeks. That is not
enough attention to the spiritual needs of the new
believer. He should be visited once a week during
that period. It is obvious that laymen must be
trained to supplement the pastor's ministry in the
care of converts.

A corps of fellowship-partners should be available at all times for assignment to one-to-one follow-up ministry. When a person receives Christ
he should be introduced to his fellowship-partner
immediately. Either the evangelism committee or
the elders could make this assignment. The fellowship-partner should report weekly to the pas-

tor or some other responsible person on the church staff as to the progress of the convert under his care.

The fellowship-partner should be trained in advance as to the philosophy and the method of the program. He must be committed to this ministry. He must also have a good working knowledge of the Bible and skill in dealing with people. Men should be assigned to men and women to women. When possible the fellowship-partner should be near the same age as the convert.

The first priority of the fellowship-partner is a covenant to pray daily for the new Christian under his care. Time devoted to study and meditation on the needs and problems encountered in the discipleship program is essential. The ministry of follow-up calls for full consecration. It will take time one would like to spend doing other things. Such a work often interferes with personal plans. The cost should be counted by those entering the program.

Tension will develop as the new convert battles with the problems he confronts. Great love and patience are needed to minister at such an hour of crisis. A fellowship-partner may sometimes feel unappreciated and will be tempted to abandon the effort. It is then one must turn to Christ and watch the incredible patience He exercised with the slow of heart among His disciples.

Twelve Week One-on-One Follow-up Procedure

Experienced people should brief new follow-up trainees as to the pressure points they may encounter and how best to cope with them. This ministry may be the most important thing to happen in the life of the new Christian between his conversion and heaven. If it is that important, give it your very best effort. One good resource is *Learning to Live* and has been included in the back of this book. It covers twelve important areas where new converts need instruction and help.

Prayer

No convert can survive without praying. Most of them really do not know how to pray. The very fact that they are Christians gives them both the right to pray and the capacity to pray.

This may be accomplished by your own prayer ministry. Always have prayer with the new convert every time you meet with him. Teach him the importance of prayer by the value you place on it.

Take him with you to prayer meeting so he may become aware of the church's corporate ministry of prayer.

Talk about prayer especially in the first few sessions. Find out if he has any problems with prayer. Teach him what the Bible says about prayer. Give him encouraging promises to read.

It would be helpful to give him a tract or a small paperback book that deals with prayer.

Encourage him to pray aloud in your presence. Many new converts have difficulty praying aloud before others. Your partner will need help to resolve this problem.

Bible Reading and Study

Make certain the disciple has a Bible to read. Inexpensive copies of Scripture portions of the New Testament or the whole Bible are available from a Bible Society. Keep a supply on hand so that everyone who receives Christ as Savior may immediately have the Word of God in their hands.

Read the Bible every time you meet with the new convert. The Word of God is a living force and will penetrate the newly awakened spiritual nature of the babe in Christ. It will feed his soul. The recent convert should never be left with the idea that the Bible is just a textbook for study. He must be taught to love, reverence and hunger for the Bible.

Not only does the fellowship-partner teach by what he says, his attitude and actions must provide an example of Christian conduct and love for the disciple to follow.

The new disciple will need to learn both how to read and how to study the Bible. Someone has wisely said that we cannot know what the Bible teaches until we know what the Bible says.

The new believer usually has no idea where to begin reading the Bible. Start with an uncompli-

cated Scripture which he can more readily understand. Getting a good start will prevent discouragement. It would be helpful if you would suggest
a plan for Bible reading. *Learning to Live* includes a
simple Bible-reading program.

Scripture Memory

Encourage the memorizing of Scripture. The
fellowship-partner should learn all the memory
passages in the twelve lessons and additional passages. The new believer will be challenged to
learn by his teacher's example. A part of each
weekly session should be devoted to memory
work. Discuss the passages and answer any questions he may have raised as to the meaning of
these verses. The practical and spiritual value of
memorizing Scripture cannot be overestimated.
To start learning the Scriptures as a new Christian
establishes a practice of edification that will enrich
the converts's walk with Christ for the rest of his
life.

The Follow-up Lessons

In each weekly session a time block should be
given to the Bible lesson in the follow-up booklet,
Learning to Live. The discipler should know these
lessons well enough to enlarge the understanding
of the convert as they discuss the passages together. Take time for the new believer's questions,
considering each one seriously. Remember most
converts have no background in Bible knowledge
or doctrine. What seems obvious to you is both

strange and difficult for him. Patience is the first virtue of a fellowship-partner.

Listen for areas of concern or need as the convert shares his own comprehension of the material. Perhaps he is having difficulty believing that his sins are really forgiven. The fellowship-partner can take this opportunity to introduce supporting Scripture passages to build the convert's faith for forgiveness and assurance. A word of personal testimony on the part of the fellowship-partner may be helpful. How did you find peace and assurance?

Never leave a new disciple without praying with him. He needs to learn that prayer is normal for true Christians. The practice of prayer teaches the vital place prayer has in maintaining the spiritual life. Encourage him to pray.

Introduce the Church

Invite the new convert to the next regular church service. Offer to go with him or her to church. One difficult hurdle for new Christians is to establish the habit of church attendance. It brings about a major change in lifestyle. The discipleship process must help new believers through this stage of spiritual development.

A part of the discipleship process is to teach new Christians some of the norms of the Christian life. Going to church is a norm. The fellowship-partner should share with this new friend the attractiveness of gathering with the people of God around the Lord Jesus Christ. The believer who has not been taught to gather with the saints when they meet in His name is a subnormal Christian. He has been short-changed spiritually by this lack. The essential ministries of the church have been denied him. No group or organization can serve as a substitute for the church.

People who come to Christ from a non-church background will need help in understanding the importance of the church to their new life in Christ. Others may have become disillusioned with the church and need guidance in sorting out the difference between dead institutionalism and the vitality of a true New Testament church.

The consistent church attendance of the fellowship-partner will help the new convert adjust to church life and activity.

Other Follow-up Steps

A weekly visit may not be sufficient for some disciples. Some people have special problems in their background that will require additional time for counsel and guidance. A convert from the drug culture may need more support and personal attention than a person who was reared in the church and traditionally observes acceptable behavior patterns. A part of the price of discipleship is to give the love and understanding troubled souls sometimes need. Be available.

Develop Friendship

Every effort must be made by the mature Christian to form a bond of true friendship with the new believer he wishes to disciple. The convert must be given time to develop trust in his discipler. He must not get the impression that all this attention is given to fulfill a religious duty on the part of his spiritual teacher. That new believer must be able to sense that his fellowship-partner is ministering to him out of true friendship and love.

The love of Christ can be manifest by the fellowship-partner in always being available. Being open and available does not mean pushy. He must respect the privacy of the disciple to whom he ministers. The fellowship-partner needs to pray constantly for the fruits of the Holy Spirit necessary for ministry that shows loving concern.

Watch for Crisis Moments

Efforts at discipleship are not always successful. Those who profess faith in Christ may resist the command to follow Him. Luke preserves from the ministry of Jesus the account of three such respondents:

> As they were walking along the road, a man said to him, "I will follow you wherever you go."
> Jesus replied, "Foxes have holes and birds of the air have nests, but the Son of Man has no place to lay his head."
> He said to another man, "Follow me."
> But the man replied, "Lord, first let me go and bury my father."
> Jesus said to him, "Let the dead bury their

own dead, but you go and proclaim the kingdom of God."

Still another said, "I will follow you, Lord; but first let me go back and say good-by to my family."

Jesus replied, "No one who puts his hand to the plow and looks back is fit for service in the kingdom of God." (Luke 9:57-62)

The crucial test of conversion comes at the point of obeying the call to discipleship. There must be no compromise at that point. The call to discipleship recognizes the absolute Lordship of Jesus Christ. It rejects the notion that personal trust in Christ is just a desirable arrangement for solving problems and getting things from God. To trust Christ fully is to follow Him at any cost. It requires a glad submission to Christ.

On another occasion Jesus preached a sermon on the Bread of Life which offended some of His disciples. "From this time many of his disciples turned back and no longer followed him" (John 6:66). Plain truth about the nature of biblical salvation will turn away the shallow professors of salvation.

The tragic practice of making discipleship palatable can only produce false disciples. All who accept the Savior with sincerity must be confronted with the implications of Christ's Lordship and with the foundational truths that build a solid Christian walk. If failure occurs with these spiritual choices, the convert will fall away. Those re-

sponsible for follow-up must exhaust every effort
to guide the convert through this crisis. It requires
much prayer and patience. Do not be too quick in
the judgment that a disciple will not make it spiritually. Go the second mile to instruct and encourage him.

Endnotes

1. *Keswick Week*, 1965, p. 156.

Chapter 5

The Church Disciples

The discipleship process requires the ministry of a mature Christian to the new believer on an individual basis, but the process also calls for the ministry of the total church to that new Christian. The services and ministries of the church should provide an atmosphere conducive to spiritual growth. Cold, formal services will not promote the growth of new believers. Nor will quarreling churches contribute to their welfare. Perhaps the most deadening effect is an attitude of indifference to new believers. Local church leadership should seek to promote a healthy climate for discipleship.

Since the local church is essentially people, the correction of the church's spiritual atmosphere must begin with the spiritual condition of each member of the fellowship. Such qualities as concern, warmth and enthusiasm cannot be generated by programming. These qualities flow from lives filled with the love of Christ.

Enlightened believers understand their obligation to the total body of believers. They see themselves as members one to another. True *koinonia*
exists because each member denies self and seeks
the best for every other member. This is divine
love in action. Fellowship resting on the founda-
tion of such love is rich and meets the deep needs
of the soul. In this atmosphere of true fellowship
the new believer discovers for herself the value of
being in the community of God's people. It will
cure one of the spiritual arrogance of going it
alone. The new believer will eagerly seek a place
in the body.

Ministries

The total discipleship program of a local church
must not only give attention to the atmosphere of
the meetings and fellowship of the body. Care
must be taken to provide ministries that meet the
needs of new believers. Mature Christians who
have become merely spectators are often spoiled
in their tastes and want only the kinds of ministries that meet their needs. If the pastor preaches a
basic message on salvation, they complain that
they are not being fed. In order for a local church
to have an effective ministry to new converts this
problem must be faced. Actually, "mature" believers who complain are not mature in the New Testament sense. Those who have grown up in Christ
find delight in ministering to new Christians.

The pulpit ministry should regularly devote
some time to instructing new converts in founda-

tional truth. The Christian education program needs classes especially designed for discipling new believers. Social gatherings of the church provide another important area for people who have just made a radical change in their social life by becoming Christians.

Every aspect of corporate church life may be strange to a recent convert. The idea of corporate prayer may be especially difficult for him. The church does well to provide special assistance to those entering the experience of corporate prayer for the first time. The well-stated prayers of older believers may make the new believer feel that he is not worthy or able to pray in the presence of others of the church.

The elders could assume the responsibility of introducing new converts to the prayer life of the church. An elder with great patience and understanding could be assigned to meet with new converts each week and teach them how to pray aloud in the gathering of believers.

This procedure is more readily carried out if after the Bible study the congregation is divided into small groups for prayer. Two groups are probably needed, one especially for recent converts. This latter group should provide a relaxed atmosphere so the new Christian does not hesitate to ask questions about prayer. Instruction should be given and each individual encouraged to offer a simple prayer in his own words.

The elder in charge of group one will have to sense when the convert has progressed to the

point of entering prayer group two. The second
prayer group acts as a bridge from the introductory experience of corporate prayer to the ad-
vanced experience of prayer in the assembly. The
value of this group is the opportunity for new believers to get used to praying aloud before others
in a context of other new believers and under the
instruction of an understanding leader. The time
block for prayer discipleship may vary with the
individual involved. A minimum of three weeks in
each basic prayer group should be recommended
before the new convert be encouraged to select
any adult prayer group he may want. If a new disciple is to become a growing disciple, learning to
pray both in private and in public is essential.

The church as a body ministers to its members.
At the beginning of his new life a convert is not
yet equipped to minister. He must be ministered
to by the assembly. Church leaders often adhere
to the premise that a convert can be retained by
putting him to work in the church. The fruit of
this procedure can be seen in the disillusionment
and discouragement of the new Christian. It is not
a job in the church that he needs; he needs to be
discipled. If the discipleship process is followed
through, the new Christian will eventually be a
solid worker. A worker must be mature and well
prepared. The best worker is the one who has
been best discipled.

The church has an *obligation* to care for new
converts. The Scottish expositor, William Barclay,
says:

The church is as responsible for the new con-
vert as the parent is for the child; and, if the
church neglects that responsibility, the church is
just as culpable as the parents who neglect the
paternal obligation within the sphere of the
home. Too often there is far too little effort to
maintain a living contact with the new entrant
into the Christian faith and the church. [1]

The church also has the *capability* to care for
new converts. It is the only divinely appointed
agency for this care. Within the prescribed ministries of the church can be found the elements most
needed in a new Christian's life. The Holy Spirit
inspired Paul to record the exact elements of apostolic church life which resulted in such successful
discipleship of new converts.

For this reason, when I could stand it no
longer, I sent to find out about your faith. I was
afraid that in some way the tempter might have
tempted you and our efforts might have been use-
less.

But Timothy has just now come to us from
you and has brought good news about your faith
and love. He has told us that you always have
pleasant memories of us and that you long to see
us, just as we also long to see you. Therefore,
brothers, in all our distress and persecution we
were encouraged about you because of your faith.
For now we really live, since you are standing
firm in the Lord. How can we thank God

*enough for you in return for all the joy we have
in the presence of our God because of you? Night
and day we pray most earnestly that we may see
you again and supply what is lacking in your
faith.*

*Now may our God and Father himself and
our Lord Jesus clear the way for us to come to
you. May the Lord make your love increase and
overflow for each other and for everyone else,
just as ours does for you. May he strengthen your
hearts so that you will be blameless and holy in
the presence of our God and Father when our
Lord Jesus comes with all his holy ones.* (1 Thessalonians 3:5-13)

Paul's Concern for Converts

The anxiety of Paul as to the progress of this
fledgling church reveals the heart of a true pastor.
Paul was deeply concerned because he had not
heard from the new Christians at Thessalonica.
He could stand the anxiety no longer so he commissioned Timothy to investigate their spiritual
condition. In addition to his practical concern for
them, Paul also gave himself to prayer. Some of
the best substantive teaching on soul-care available to us is found in the recorded prayer of Paul
on behalf of his converts. Here we learn the pressure point. What were his concerns for these new
Christians?

Paul prayed first of all that he might be able to
see the Thessalonians so that he could minister to

them. He knew how Satan seeks to keep the shepherds from the sheep, so he prayed about the mere mechanics of reaching these newborn souls.

He prayed directly that what was lacking in their faith might be completed. The difficiencies of their spiritual life were taken to God in prayer. Paul poured out his heart in intercession for the maturity of those he had led to Christ.

The level of prayer ministry in a congregation has a bearing on its ability to do follow-up. A prayerless church will have serious difficulty offering care to new converts. In our concern for improved methodology prayer should not be forgotten. Prayer can be replaced by nothing else.

The bulk of recorded prayer in the New Testament centers on the growth and development of new Christians. The high priestly prayer of our Lord has inherent in it this concept. The end product of redemption is what counts. Prayer has a bearing on the production of that desirable end product—a person perfect in Christ.

Prayer is not tacked on to the follow-up of converts for the sake of piety. Prayer is a working part of the total program and should be given a larger place than it frequently enjoys.

Each petition in the prayer of Paul for new Christians touches some area critical to their spiritual growth.

I have not stopped giving thanks for you, remembering you in my prayers. I keep asking that the God of our Lord Jesus Christ, the glori-

ous Father, may give you the Spirit of wisdom and revelation, so that you may know him better. I pray also that the eyes of your heart may be enlightened in order that you may know the hope to which he has called you, the riches of his glorious inheritance in the saints, and his incomparably great power for us who believe. That power is like the working of his mighty strength, which he exerted in Christ when he raised him from the dead and seated him at his right hand in the heavenly realms, far above all rule and authority, power and dominion, and every title that can be given, not only in the present age but also in the one to come. And God placed all things under his feet and appointed him to be head over everything for the church, which is his body, the fullness of him who fills everything in every way. (Ephesians 1:16-23)

For this reason I kneel before the Father, from whom his whole family in heaven and on earth derives its name. I pray that out of his glorious riches he may strengthen you with power through his Spirit in your inner being, so that Christ may dwell in your hearts through faith. And I pray that you, being rooted and established in love, may have power, together with all the saints, to grasp how wide and long and high and deep is the love of Christ, and to know this love that surpasses knowledge—that you may be filled to the measure of all the fullness of God. (Ephesians 3:14-19)

For this reason, since the day we heard about you, we have not stopped praying for you and asking God to fill you with the knowledge of his will through all spiritual wisdom and understanding. And we pray this in order that you may live a life worthy of the Lord and may please him in every way: bearing fruit in every good work, growing in the knowledge of God, being strengthened with all power according to his glorious might so that you may have great endurance and patience, and joyfully giving thanks to the Father, who has qualified you to share in the inheritance of the saints in the kingdom of light. For he has rescued us from the dominion of darkness and brought us into the kingdom of the Son he loves, in whom we have redemption, the forgiveness of sins.

He is the image of the invisible God, the firstborn over all creation. For by him all things were created: things in heaven and on earth, visible and invisible, whether thrones or powers or rulers or authorities; all things were created by him and for him. He is before all things, and in him all things hold together. And he is the head of the body, the church; he is the beginning and the firstborn from among the dead, so that in everything he might have the supremacy. (Colossians 1:9-18)

A group of spiritually mature believers should be commissioned in every church to especially intercede for new converts. The training material for this group can be found in the Pauline prayers. How should prayer groups pray for new believers? The petitions of the apostle Paul are just as relevant to modern converts as they were to the converts of the first century. The great burdens that pour from the Spirit-taught heart of Paul should be the heart burdens of today's intercessor.

Paul's Nine Petitions

The prayers of Paul contain at least nine petitions for new believers. Perhaps the prayer group by in-depth study of these passages will discover other important petitions to add to their intercession.

1. Pray for new believers to have a good understanding of the rich blessings of salvation. To know their privileges in Christ will help them grow in grace.

2. Pray that converts may be empowered by the Holy Spirit so that Christ may dwell in their hearts by faith. This petition touches every important aspect of the deeper life.

3. Pray that converts may learn how to walk in righteousness.

4. Pray that they may bear fruit by doing good works.

5. Pray that new Christians may become established in Christ.

6. Pray that they who have come to Christ may learn both patience in trial and joy in trust.

7. Pray that the newborn babes in Christ may learn the full meaning of their deliverance from Satan so they may live as overcomers.

8. Pray that they may have a good understanding of the Church as the Body of Christ where they may live and minister.

9. Pray that they will understand the headship of Christ over all things and in particular their own lives.

Small Groups and the Follow-up Ministry

The concepts of follow-up ministry are not a twentieth-century innovation. This can be demonstrated by the follow-up program mandated by Christ Himself in the Great Commission put into action by the early church. From the days of the first century until now there has attended all church growth some workable kind of follow-up program. The program is really how you put the principles to work. Unfortunately, pastors and churches sometimes try to initiate programs when they have not understood the principles which produced those programs. When once the biblical principles are understood the Holy Spirit will give assistance in the application of those principles.

Many church historians believe that the Methodist revival was the most prolonged revival of the Church since the Reformation. The continued moving of God's Spirit in the growth of this movement has often been attributed to the very successful method developed for the care of new converts. While this methodology was developed and put in use over 200 ago it is worthy of consideration by contemporary Christians.

John Wesley developed with each of his societies, or what we would call congregations, a system of class meetings. In today's nomenclature these would be called *small groups* within the larger overall church family. Modern church people are attempting to cover this important concept of giving to the new believer a small unit to which she can relate and develop spiritually while becoming a part of the larger church body. The Methodist class meeting was designed to do just that.

Mature, godly men were selected by the church to lead the classes. It was required that every new convert enroll in such a class. His faithful attendance in the class meeting was regularly checked by the church leadership. In fact, if he had neglected attendance at the class meeting he could be barred from the Lord's table until he had a legitimate reason for not attending, or until he resumed his regular attendance at the class meetings. It was required that he should attend three out of every four meetings in order to be eligible for communion. Cards were given out to those who attended as evidence that they had been at the class meeting.

Modern evangelicals often believe that regulations and records are the death of spirituality. History demonstrates that the absence of regulations and records are more likely to cause death. Those early Spirit-filled Methodists saw great value in regulations and also in records. Meticulous records were kept of attendance at the class meetings and spiritual records as to the development and maturation of each Christian.

Perhaps the most famous Methodist class leader was Mr. William Reeves of the Lambeth Society not far from London, England. His remarkable story was published in 1853. He had at that time concluded thirty-four years as an active class leader. His church affectionately called him Father Reeves, for he was indeed a father to newborn souls. He in a biblical manner gave of his time and strength to the nurture of the lambs in the Lambeth Society.

His class met every Lord's Day afternoon sharply at 2 o'clock. The meeting was deliberately designed to help Christians grow. Father Reeves would select those hymns that taught spiritual truths most needed by his class at that time. After the singing of the hymns and prayer he would then give himself to exhortation and the asking of questions. Direct, pointed questions were asked of believers present regarding the progress made in their own spiritual lives and also regarding the struggles they may have been encountering regarding the world, the flesh and the devil. This was followed by helpful instruction from the Word of God.

Father Reeves spent part of every class teaching basic doctrine. However, he did not overlook practical truths like stewardship and the problems of interpersonal relationships among Christians.

The benefit of the class meeting to the new Christians was not only in the content of the meeting, but in the prayerful concern of the class leader for them as individuals. Not only did Father Reeves lead the class meeting, but he spent many hours visiting each member of his class. He rose early in the morning to wait before God for long periods of intercession on behalf of those for whom he had been given the responsibility of ministry.

William Reeves was not an ordained minister. He was an ordinary layman and a hardworking man who spent as many hours at his job as any other man in the community. His ministry to the class meeting was done on his own time and at great personal expense. No one ever had to explain to the new Christians at Lambeth that there was someone who cared for them. They just knew that Father Reeves had concern. It is not surprising to learn that there were very few dropouts from the Methodist classes in the Lambeth Society.

What worked at Lambeth worked all cross Britain and across North America wherever the Methodist church went to minister. A revival blessing was sustained in the movement for almost a century. The class meeting concept had much to do with the prolonged usefulness of the Methodist awakening.

The principles employed in the class meeting are sound, not only from a biblical viewpoint, but also psychologically. Modern behavioral sciences have discovered the value of a small group relationship. Our churches are sometimes structured to turn people out in the cold and we do not realize it. The example in Methodism should cause us to look closely at the structures within our churches. The question should be asked, "Is there a group within your church to which every new convert can relate, a place where he will find fellowship, nurture for his soul, strengthening and spiritual development, so the day may come when he too may help others as he has been helped?"

The revivals of the eighteenth century were not exclusively Methodist. Within the Church of England and the non-conformist churches the breath of new spiritual life brought many to Christ. The awakening within the Church of England was generally limited to a parish where the vicar had been filled with the Spirit and began preaching revival truth. A number of these leaders, quite independent of Methodism, created small groups for the express purpose of discipling their converts.

These examples of follow-up by means of small groups ministry have their counterpart in today's church. The heart of this method is to provide new converts with a fellowship circle small enough to be personal. An individual believer can easily be lost in the crowd of a very active evangelical church.

Qualities of personality and temperament will limit the level of close fellowship a believer may have with others. While he learns to love and appreciate the whole body of believers, certain mem-

bers will be more compatible and consequently
more helpful than others. The small group concept is not a move to fracture the fellowship into
small groups but rather to enrich the church by
providing the direct ministry of the smaller circle
of fellowship.

Small groups can become divisive when they
are formed out of a wrong philosophy of ministry.
Small groups are not substitutes for the whole assembly but one of the integral functions of the
larger group. Unless the small group relates to the
larger body it becomes an island of spiritual isola-
tionism. The small group is protected from these
evils when it is initiated by the church and is incorporated into its pastoral care.

While the small group concept can be used with
profit to help mature Christians grow and minister, it has an even greater value as a means of following up the new convert. He is less threatened
by a small group and therefore more likely to take
the first steps of vocal prayer and testimony
within this group. Sharing problems and questions encountered in his new walk as a Christian is
easier in a small group atmosphere.

Care must be taken to prevent an individual believer from using a small group as a substitute for
the church. He may be tempted to avoid the regular meetings of the assembly feeling it does not
contribute enough to his Christian life. This problem can be avoided by teaching the small group
the value of the larger assembly. The example of
church attendance on the part of the group leader

and the mature members of the group encourages the new believer to do likewise.

Small Group Formats

The format of the small group has many alternatives. The Sunday school in some instances has been the best agency for forming small groups to provide fellowship and direct one-to-one ministry. Adult classes may be divided into as many small groups as the needs of the class may require.

Home Bible studies provide another type of small group meeting that can serve both for evangelism outreach and nurture of new Christians. The home Bible study should never be a substitute for the biblical studies program of the church. It is a supplementary program feeding its results into the regular church program.

Small groups can be formed in a geographical area. Suppose five families live in a housing development. This could be the core group. New converts in that area would be incorporated into the group. One midwest congregation divides its entire congregation into such neighborhood groups and assigns elders to give oversight.

There are no hard and fast rules for forming small groups. The needs and the composition of each church is different. Leadership under the guidance of the Holy Spirit must develop the kind of small group ministry that best fits each church.

The proper use of the small group may prove to be the best way to integrate a new Christian into the life of the assembly.

Church Membership and Follow-up

The Pauline epistles give a rather complete cross section of apostolic church practice with regard to the members of local churches. I can almost hear someone say, "What members? Did they have membership in the early church?" For some reason the idea has gotten around that the church in her days of purity was not encumbered with the problems of membership. The time has come to set the record straight with regard to this subject.

The starting point for this discussion is the nature of the Church. It is a body made up of many members. The apostle Paul explained to new Christians that by spiritual experience they were a part of the Body of Christ. He also was quick to explain that their function in that body could take place only within the context of a local assembly. So, the church for them was that gathering of believers when they met for preaching, prayer, the breaking of bread and fellowship.

Does the New Testament indicate that the apostolic assemblies had a means of identifying members? This writer believes that it does; a number of passages make reference to the reception policies practiced in Paul's day. The epistles reflect some standard forms in the government, finance and basis of fellowship in the congregations founded by the apostles. Local churches were not "mixed multitudes" made up of any who chose to identify with them. Each local church reserved the right to "receive" those worthy of fellowship.

For all practical purposes their procedure is identical with the concept of church membership practiced by most evangelical churches today. The early church was not nearly so unstructured as some would have us believe. As Christians traveled from one area to another they carried with them letters of commendation from their local assemblies. Admission to the Lord's Supper and other privileges of assembly life were apparently restricted to those with an established testimony. A stranger was required to produce credentials.

A sample of such a letter is found in Romans:

> *I commend to you our sister Phoebe, a servant of the church in Cenchrea. I ask you to receive her in the Lord in a way worthy of the saints and to give her any help she may need from you, for she has been a great help to many people, including me.* (Romans 16:1-2)

Paul gave Epaphroditus a similar commendation in his epistle to the church at Philippi.

> *Welcome him in the Lord with great joy, and honor men like him, because he almost died for the work of Christ, risking his life to make up for the help you could not give me.* (Philippians 2:29-30)

Active members of the assembly were properly received as such when their testimony and manner of life had been verified. The elders looked for

evidence of God's grace in them. Such a procedure was necessary to safeguard the local church
from false doctrine and carnal living. The darkest
periods of the Church's history have come when
the unconverted have been welcomed to membership with the hope they would eventually be
saved. This is an unscriptural practice.

It is equally unscriptural to have no membership at all. Every Bible-believing church should
have a membership policy based on the Word of
God. The local church should look upon new converts becoming church members as a normal follow-up of their conversion. The souls won to
Christ must in a very real and visible way become
clearly identified both before sinners and saints as
a member of a local church.

In addition to the scriptural reasons for church
membership there are practical reasons for a
strong policy on church membership. Christians
who refrain from joining the church have reserva-
tions regarding the congregation and its practice.
Their loyalty is limited. Full commitment to the
ministry of the church is lacking. Such believers
are selective in both their stewardship and service.
Some adherents appear to be as loyal as members
but a closer look will prove that they are not.

Church-building programs afford a good example of the limited loyalty of adherents. Our
churches often face difficulty in securing financ-
ing because forty to fifty percent of the congregation is made up of adherents. Adherents do not
vote or sign mortgages. The small membership

may feel hesitant to step into a building expansion program when they are a bare majority or in some instances less than a majority of the congregation. The ultimate growth of such a church becomes seriously limited by a poor membership policy. Its evangelistic goals may never be realized because the membership policy places such serious limitations on its resources for workers and finances.

The local churches were admonished by Paul to exercise discipline over their members. Incidents of immorality, division, insubordination and false doctrine occurred among members in the early church. Appropriate action was taken by church leadership to discipline such members.

Christian stewardship is another practical reason for urging all the believers worshiping with a given church to become a part of its membership. Adherents tend to be selective in their giving to the church. They respond to special appeals and to many outside organizations very readily. The general operational cost of a local church does not appeal to them. They leave the major responsibility for the budget to the members while they give the major share of their money to favorite projects.

Next to stewardship, service should be given priority by the Christian. Service is inherent in the Christian life and the church is the normal center of service for the believer. The very nature of Christian service requires lines of authority. The cause of evangelism has been greatly confused by self-styled Christian service that boasts of its non-church stand. To be an active member of a live New Testament church offers effective channels of ministry to the believer. The local church guides, oversees and trains for Christian service.

The membership of the church has always carried with it both privileges and responsibilities. There is a vast difference between people who just attend the services of the church and those who by the new birth are actually members of the Body of Christ. Privilege is extended only to those received as true believers.

> *Accept one another, then, just as Christ accepted you, in order to bring praise to God.* (Romans 15:7)

Endnotes

1. William Barclay, *Turning to God* (Grand Rapids, MI: Baker Book House, 1975 ed.), p. 82.

Chapter 6

How Long Does It Take to Make a Disciple?

Follow-up programs should be designed with a time frame long enough to complete the work of disciple-making. If a pastor and his lay leadership are concerned about developing a credible program of discipleship, serious consideration should be given to the implications of the question, "How long does it take to make a disciple?"

Our culture has been oriented to think in terms of rapid results and instant production of anything that it needs. Disciples are not produced instantly. It takes time and effort to build into a life the qualities necessary to maturity. The Lord Jesus Christ spent three and one-half years discipling the twelve men who were to be the foundational apostles for the Church. He gave to them the major portion of His time for those years. He spent hours each day in teaching, preaching and talking with the disciples. They were exposed to His methods firsthand. The very best procedures for discipleship were employed by the Lord Jesus Christ, but this did not hurry up the process.

It is interesting that it took a similar period of time to disciple the apostle Paul. He indicates that after his conversion he went to Arabia for prayer and meditation in preparation for his future ministry. Then, three years later he went down and spent fifteen days with Peter and the church leadership in Jerusalem for the final touches on his discipleship. Barnabas was also involved in helping disciple this man, but altogether a minimum of three years was spent in preparing Paul, the great missionary evangelist of the apostolic church.

Leroy Eims, a representative of Navigators, estimates that from convert to disciple requires two years; from disciple to worker, an additional two years; from worker to leader, an additional three years.[1]

By Eims' estimate, the time required to disciple and bring a person to useful leadership is seven years. There is much to be said for his conclusions.

It takes time to develop leadership that is spiritually mature and doctrinally competent to lead. The dirth of leadership in the contemporary church is related directly to the poor methods of discipleship. In many churches the discipleship program is little more than the distributing of a few tracts and a copy of the Scripture, and holding a few classes in preparation for baptism; then the believer is left to fend for himself with very little guidance from that point on. The end result of this procedure is a believer who never reaches his full potential and who never matures to the level that he can become an active worker and useful leader in the assembly.

Good discipleship methods will produce all the leadership any church will ever need. The gifts have been placed in the body. Those gifts must be brought into action by good training and teaching and the encouragement of God's people to serve.

The time sequences suggested in Eims' book for discipleship may seem too much for some, but serious consideration must be given to an adequate time span to train fruitful disciples.

The first three months of the discipleship program may be occupied with a fellowship-partner activity and a study of *Learning to Live*. During that period of time, the fellowship-partner should introduce the believer to the life of the church. He should give the convert a tract on water baptism and explain the ordinances of the church.

In the final stages of this twelve-week period, the groundwork should be laid for moving that convert into the pastor's membership class. This would be further preparation for water baptism and being received into the active membership of the church. This stage of discipleship will take at least another two months. But the program must not end there. These five months have only introduced this new Christian to the wonderful and exciting life in Christ Jesus and in the service of His church.

The new convert should then move from the
membership class into a six-week class on missions awareness. He has already been introduced
to personal soul winning and has had impressed
upon him the need for getting involved and perhaps by this time has been instrumental in bringing some people to Christ. The time has now
come to introduce him to world missions, to give
him a larger vision, to help him see the importance
of intercessory prayer and his own stewardship
commitments to sending the gospel to the ends of
the earth.

During these first six months the new Christian
will have gained some basic tools for his own
study and development. At this point in time, he
should be introduced to some small group if he
has not already been involved in one. The small
group will provide an atmosphere for his initial efforts at serving others. It will help him to learn the
art of fellowship and it will draw his attention to
the fact that he is a member of the body and as
such has responsibility to the other members of
that body. Sharing will be an enriching experience
for him spiritually. However, the ministry of the
small group should not replace the continued
training for Christian life and ministry.

The convert should be encouraged to enroll in a
basic Bible study course in the adult Sunday
school. This should be a book study, if possible.
At the completion of the book study, he should
enroll in the doctrinal course to get a broader understanding of basic Christian doctrine. With this

step the first full year of the convert's discipleship program is complete. He should now be a functioning member of the church and regularly participating in its life. He should be feeding his own heart from the Word and have at least a working knowledge of essential doctrines.

The next step is to acquaint him more thoroughly with personal evangelism. Enroll him in a soul winner's course, which will give him a basic understanding of the content of the gospel message, the steps in salvation and an acquaintance with the problems of those people to whom he will be bringing the gospel witness. After the content course is completed, the convert should be assigned to an elder or some other mature Christian to do house-to-house visitation or some other form of direct evangelism so that he is actually learning experientially how to carry out this kind of ministry.

A good, solid book study such as the book of Romans would be very appropriate at this stage in the Christian's development. This new disciple should be encouraged to get involved in a home Bible study conducted by a spiritually mature person from the church. People differ in the amount of time and the interest they have in study, and it is important to provide enough alternatives so that the person who is particularly ambitious in this area may have ample opportunity to apply himself in the study of the Word of God.

The time has come in the discipleship program to impress upon this new convert the importance of serving the Lord Jesus Christ and that being a Christian is to be a member of the body, and being a member of the body one is responsible to minister to the edification and building up of that body. A course on the gifts and how to recognize his gifts might be appropriate here. Perhaps those who work closest with the new disciple will have discovered certain aptitudes and abilities and may recommend the particular area of the church's work where he would best fit. One will have gifts for teaching or leadership while another may show a gift of helps and be able to minister to the needs of people or to the physical needs of the church building. Leadership must discern and attempt to guide new disciples into some kind of Christian service. The area of Christian service selected will dictate the next steps in training. A new disciple should be encouraged to enroll in the course of study that will prepare him for effective ministry.

Advancing the Disciple to Worker

Jesus prepared His disciples for ministry by instruction and commission. Instructing preceded the commissioning. The nature of the instruction Jesus gave is revealed in the two Greek words employed by Matthew in 10:5 and 11:1 of his Gospel. The word *parangelas* means to order, direct, advise. The word *diataso* means to order, direct, command. The instructions then were related to the work the disciples were about to do. They were to carry out the directives of Jesus in their ministry. The doctrinal input had already been given to them. The instruction on this occasion was practical and prepared the disciples to become workers for Christ.

This passage records the first apprenticeship of the apostles. A comparison of the four Gospels would indicate that Jesus dispatched them on more than one mission in order to develop their abilities in ministry. While the Gospels of Mark and Luke add some details to the basic instructions, the Matthew passage sets the pattern for instructing new workers for their first experience in ministry.

The continued use of these two Greek words in the epistles indicates the early Church used the method of Jesus in preparing disciples to become workers. The authoritative directives of the apostles regarding the work of the Church were given to new workers. Titus was instructed as to the pattern for organizing the assemblies in Crete.

> *The reason I left you in Crete was that you might straighten out what was left unfinished and appoint elders in every town, as I directed you.* (Titus 1:5)

Paul wrote to the church at Thessalonica to remind them of the instruction they had received.

> *For you know what instructions we gave you by the authority of the Lord Jesus.* (1 Thessalonians 4:2)

The word *parangelas* is translated *commandments*.
Paul made it a practice not only to teach his followers the system of Christian truth in the form of
doctrines, but following the pattern of Jesus he instructed them in the directives which give good
order to the work of God's people.

The discipleship process must ultimately reach
this level of instruction or it falls short of the New
Testament plan. Since all believers are gifted to
minister by some means to the assembly it must
be concluded that every believer is to be a worker
for Christ.

So few modern Christians ever become workers. Sunday morning church has become the
greatest spectator activity in America. Why have
so many believers been blinded to both the obligation and the privilege of working for Christ? Is it
because they have been indoctrinated but have not
been instructed in the divine directives for service?

As the pastor and lay leaders design a total
church discipleship program, attention should be
given to providing the best possible instruction for
potential workers. It should be kept in mind that
the basic follow-up steps do not constitute a full
discipleship procedure. Most follow-up programs
do not go far enough. They must lead the new
convert to established Christian living, to the fellowship and membership of the church, to open
confession of faith. But the new Christian has
been sold short if not introduced to the privilege
of seving Christ.

The gospel record gives ample insight into what constitutes appropriate instruction for disciples being prepared to become workers. In Matthew 10:5-11:1 Jesus explains the principles that are to govern this work of the disciples.

Instructions for Workers

The Lord Jesus commanded the twelve apostles to restrict their work to the Jewish population of Palestine. Those who work for Christ must observe the limitations the divine call places on them. While there are dispensational overtones in this passage a general principle can still be drawn from Christ's instruction to the twelve. New workers must be taught to sense the specific work to which the Lord is directing them. The recognition of this principle will be a safeguard against the all-too-prevalent condition of overworked Christians who have taken on more than God meant for them.

The Savior proceeds with the exact particulars of their work. The disciples were to preach, heal, cast out demons and raise the dead. Jesus had been teaching His disciples these ministries by precept and example and now He sends them forth on their own to labor. They were to do what Jesus did in His labors for the Father. Modern disciples, both clergy and lay, must learn the same principle. Those who are teachers must actually demonstrate the work they teach others to do. If new believers are to be taught personal work, their teacher must be a good personal worker.

New Christians, according to Jesus' method, are to learn the pressures of working for Christ. True commitment to follow Jesus alters the lifestyle of the layman just as it alters the lifestyle of those called to the pastoral ministry. Working for Christ can affect your income and your personal plans in a very real way. The life of faith is for all Christians. Christ was saying to the twelve that to obey His orders would place them in such jeopardy that they must learn to live in simple dependence on God.

The servants of Christ encounter very real dangers and difficulties. Jesus described for His disciples the kinds of spiritual enemies they would meet in the course of their ministry. Social, political and religious pressures will be placed on those who dare to work for Christ in this alien world. Jesus was frank to tell His followers that He was sending them out as sheep among wolves. He undergirded them with the assurance of God's intervention. They could expect the Spirit of God to give them what they needed in the hour of trial. They could also overcome by the cultivation of those qualities of character which would make them as wise as serpents and as harmless as doves. The Christian worker is to be both wise and inoffensive in her deportment. The disciple is never to generate opposition to the gospel by bad attitudes and self-vindication.

So do not be afraid of them. There is nothing concealed that will not be disclosed, or hidden that will not be made known. (Matthew 10:26)

The disciple who sets out to work for Christ should not be apprehensive about the opposition he encounters but should fix his eyes on the hope of that coming day when Christ will bring everything to light. What the disciple has learned in the comfort and security of the church he must now boldly declare to the world.

This is a critical stage in the spiritual progress of every new Christian. He is threatened by this exposure to the unsympathetic forces of a wicked world. The example of his Teacher is to be held before him as a model. The Teacher here is obviously Christ. The strongest argument for a new Christian's taking this step toward vulnerability is the fact that Christ took this step for his sake during the days of His incarnation. Christ took this risk as no other man has done in all of history. Christ counts on those of us who follow Him to gladly take this same risk.

> *Do not be afraid of those who kill the body but cannot kill the soul. Rather, be afraid of the One who can destroy both soul and body in hell. Are not two sparrows sold for a penny? Yet not one of them will fall to the ground apart from the will of your Father. And even the very hairs of your head are all numbered. So don't be afraid; you are worth more than many sparrows.*

> *Whoever acknowledges me before men, I will also acknowledge him before my Father in heaven. But whoever disowns me before men, I will disown him before my Father in heaven.* (Matthew 10:28-33)

The threat and sometimes the danger encountered by the disciple who dares to confess Christ before men is to be committed to the Father. Jesus assured His immediate disciples that God sees their plight and His care for them will be very real in the hour of their testing. The same loving Heavenly Father watches over modern disciples of the Lord Jesus Christ.

> *Do not suppose that I have come to bring peace to the earth. I did not come to bring peace, but a sword. For I have come to turn*

> *"a man against his father,*
> *a daughter against her mother,*
> *a daughter-in-law against her*
> *mother-in-law—*
> *a man's enemies will be the members*
> *of his own household."*

> *Anyone who loves his father or mother more than me is not worthy of me; anyone who loves his son or daughter more than me is not worthy of me.* (Matthew 10:34-37)

Jesus made it plain that working for Him could

cause family conflict and strife. Sometimes a new convert comes from a non-Christian background and a family that probably is not sympathetic to his new life. The opposition may not be so overt until that new Christian begins to serve Christ openly and publicly. The new disciple needs to be pre-conditioned for this eventuality. The basic instructions given the new worker should caution him not to be surprised if his work causes family strife.

While the family is sacred and its welfare a major concern in the Christian system, Christ does teach the necessity of each individual making a commitment to Him that is greater than his commitment to family. The purpose of that commitment is not to generate family strife but rather to promote family good. The best possible way to win the members of one's family is by an uncompromising devotion to the Lord Jesus Christ. Until the disciple has come to this level of supreme love for Christ he or she is not yet ready to be a worker.

> *And anyone who does not take his cross and follow me is not worthy of me. Whoever finds his life will lose it, and whoever loses his life for my sake will find it.* (Matthew 10:38-39)

This passage declares the principle of self-denial as it applies to disciples who are sent to work for Christ. The central truth in the life of self-denial is cross-bearing. In every biblical context the cross is identified with death. This passage is no exception. Disciples who dare to face the world and take up the work of the gospel must die to their own self-interests.

Verse 39 describes cross-bearing as losing one's life for the sake of Christ. Jesus was not necessarily speaking of martyrdom in this verse. A disciple can lose his life without physically dying. He may lose his life by discounting the importance of his own comforts, profits, privileges and pleasures in favor of a life devoted to the work and the worship of Christ. The demands of Christ's work supersede the demands of his own interests.

A casual consideration of this principle may make it appear harsh, but a true understanding of it reveals the goodness of God. The life of self-denial as taught in this context is not morbid. Christ presents the life of self-denial as whole, free and rewarding. It is essential to success in the work of the Lord. Most believers who begin to minister and then drop out of ministry do so because of the conflict of self-interest. Those who oversee the discipleship process should make sure the new Christian has come to an understanding of this basic principle of the Christian life.

> *He who receives you receives me, and he who receives me receives the one who sent me. Anyone who receives a prophet because he is a prophet will receive a prophet's reward, and anyone who receives a righteous man because he is a righteous man will receive a righteous man's reward.*

And if anyone gives even a cup of cold water to one of these little ones because he is my disciple, I tell you the truth, he will certainly not lose his reward. (Matthew 10:40-42)

The final directive Jesus gave the twelve disciples instructed them to keep in mind the reward that Christ will give some day. The smallest act of human kindness done for Christ is a work worthy of eternal reward. The disciple is taught to minister unstintingly without regard for reward from people now but anticipating the reward given by Christ in the world to come.

Another very subtle principle can be found in this passage. The disciple is identified with Christ. The treatment he receives is the treatment of Christ and His cause on earth. There is a vast difference between the reactions of ungodly people which the disciple brings on himself and those reactions that are brought about by his identification with Jesus Christ.

Jesus did not mean to teach that the response to gospel proclamation and other forms of Christian work would always meet opposition. Christ taught His disciples to look for good responses and to rejoice in them. Therefore, the Christian worker should receive all kindness as coming to him for Christ's sake.

This passage is very reassuring to the new disciple. He now understands that the work of the gospel does not always produce strife, persecution and other adverse reactions. The work of the gospel will be received by many and attended with love, hospitality and kindness.

Care should be taken to point out this prospect to the disciple about to undertake some work assignment for Christ. Some Christians have only comprehended the possibility of the negative reaction. They are always on their guard and expectant of the negative reactions on the part of the world. This is an unhealthy attitude. Disciples should know how to handle the adverse when it comes, but should always be anticipating a cup of refreshing cold water rather than the storm of persecution.

Jesus' Four-Step Method

Four steps can be discerned in Jesus' method of making disciples into workers. They were first taught the conceptual truth they needed to understand the work of Christ. It is at this point that the modern approach often stops, and because it fails in taking all the steps necessary to producing workers the effort fails. The new disciple is left in a state of frustration.

Christ went beyond teaching to training. Having furnished His disciples with essential doctrine He proceeded to train them by example. The disciples lived and traveled with Jesus and consequently observed firsthand the Savior's work. They learned by on-the-job training. The Master provided the ideal model.

The method of Jesus did not stop with training. He also instructed the trainee in the principles he needed to understand and apply as a worker.

These directives were absolutely essential to the worker's success. The directives Jesus gave these potential workers were largely related to their commitment. They spelled out the exact nature of commitment required of workers for Christ.

The fourth step in Jesus' method of discipling workers was to commission them to a specific task. They were sent to the work. Jesus did not distribute a sheet to check over preferences for work. He sent His disciples. The prerogative to send workers today rests with the church. Believers who have been convinced they ought to work for Christ are often forced to design their own commission and that procedure has been far from satisfactory. When the disciple has chosen his own work he may feel that he alone can evaluate and oversee it.

Some real spiritual tragedies have resulted from this method. A good and godly person sought to serve, but his church lacked the insight and system to train him and put him to work. So he carved out his own kingdom without the needed guidance and oversight of the brotherhood. He became a law unto himself, critical of all other Christian work. He was blind to his mistakes and reacted to any effort to correct them. The work was his work and not the Lord's or the church's. This disciple's story would have read differently had the church discipled him and then commissioned him to the work. Church leadership can counsel the disciple as to areas of need in the total church ministry and guide the new disciple into work which fits his spiritual gifts.

Advancing the Worker to Leader

Not all workers are leaders. But some among the new believers by the distribution of the Holy Spirit have gifts of leadership. Pastors or elders may observe the qualities of leadership in some and begin the next stage of discipleship, advancing the worker to leader.

One cannot be a good leader who has never been a worker. The Christian who is thrust into leadership without careful discipleship as a worker will probably fail. The best education for leadership is following a good leader. Working under the oversight of one who is experienced and mature is a necessary preparation for assuming leadership.

The worker role develops the necessary disposition for leading. Workers learn the value of cooperation, team work and self-sacrifice for the sake of the body. They learn personal discipline. They learn how to overcome their failures. The fruit of the Spirit is promoted by ministry for Christ.

The elders of the church should, under the pastor's direction, be responsible for training workers for leadership. The most mature workers should be selected for leadership training. The responsibility and testings of one who leads is too much for a spiritual novice.

Disciples who are still struggling with personal problems will not survive the pressures of being leaders. New believers can suffer spiritual damage by being thrust into leadership positions before they are ready. The pattern moves from convert to disciple, from disciple to worker, from worker to leader.

Not every disciple will be a leader, but every disciple should be fully trained to minister to the Body of Christ according to his spiritual gifts. When is a disciple fully trained? By what standard can the level of training be measured? Jesus laid down a principle for determining complete training.

> *A student is not above his teacher, but everyone who is fully trained will be like his teacher.* (Luke 6:40)

The secret of good discipleship rests with the teacher. A good teacher lives the kind of Christian life that is worthy of imitating. The apostle Paul and his co-workers were such teachers.

> *[B]ecause our gospel came to you not simply with words, but also with power, with the Holy Spirit and with deep conviction. You know how we lived among you for your sake. You became imitators of us and of the Lord; in spite of severe suffering, you welcomed the message with the joy given by the Holy Spirit.* (1 Thessalonians 1:5-6)

The teacher is to so follow Christ that he can turn to his disciples and instruct them to follow him. The teacher is to be a model of a true disciple of Christ.

The scriptural plan for fully training disciples calls not only for an adequate teacher for individual follow-up but it also calls for a corporate ministry of the church to complete this process.

> *And He gave some as apostles, and some as prophets, and some as evangelists, and some as pastors and teachers, for the equipping of the saints for the work of service, to the building up of the body of Christ.* (Ephesians 4:11-12, NASB)

The Greek word *kataptismon*, translated *equipped* in Ephesians 4:12, is the same word translated *fully trained* in Luke 6:40. Disciples then are fully trained by the God-appointed ministers of the church. Preaching is essential to discipleship.

The Ephesians passage expands the measure of what it means to be fully trained. A fully trained Christian is one who has been equipped to work and one who actually serves Christ in a way that is building up the body.

The reinstatement of biblical discipleship into the life of the church will bring with it the vitality of apostolic Christianity. It will further benefit the church by providing a work force commensurate with the task of world evangelism.

There is a sense in which a Christian is a disciple all of his life, for a disciple is a learner and one is never too mature to learn. There is always something new to be learned about the Christian life and about serving Jesus Christ.

Endnotes

1. Eims, Leroy, *The Lost Art of Disciple-Making* (Grand Rapids, MI: Zondervan Publishing House, 1978).

Care of Converts
Leader's Guide

Introduction

Care of Converts is intended to be used as a training manual for local church leadership. It is written from the viewpoint that discipling is primarily a church function. While it is true that the new believer must have individual follow-up care, discipleship does not stop there. That believer must find the bridge that leads him or her to the church, or discipleship has failed. God has no other place or plan for converts than the Church, which is the Body of Christ.

Too many evangelical churches have little more than a stop-gap follow-up procedure. This can only be altered when the leadership of the church comes to understand the biblical basis of discipleship and the practical reasons for it.

Care of Converts leads the local church pastoral staff and lay leadership through the concepts of total church discipleship. The members of the executive board, the elders and the deacons, the Christian education workers and the evangelism committee could all profit from this study.

Teaching the leadership the basic principles of discipleship is the first step in preparing the whole congregation for building a solid ongoing ministry of follow-up.

Each member of the class should have his or her individual copy of the textbook, *Care of Converts*. The lesson should be read in advance of the class and important ideas and questions underscored so the student will be ready for class involvement.

The Leader's Guide has been prepared with the teacher or discussion leader in mind. Each lesson has four features designed to aid the teacher in the study and presentation of the lesson.

The *objective of the lesson* summarizes its purpose. The *group activities* section suggests a variety of approaches that may be used in presenting the lesson. The questions for discussion will help both the teacher and the student discover the important issues in each lesson.

A key Scripture passage from each chapter has been selected for an in-depth study. A good reference Bible or commentary will assist the teacher in developing an exposition of the passage. Care should be taken to relate the biblical study to the *objective of the lesson*. Encourage student participation by occasionally having a member of the class prepare the *Biblical Basis of Discipleship* section and present it to the class.

The overall purpose of this manual is to establish the need for the care of new converts and to instruct the leadership in the principles of such a ministry. A closely related objective is to train among the leaders a team of disciplers skilled in dealing individually with new believers.

The manual focuses on the need for church-oriented discipleship. The teacher or discussion leader can make the course more meaningful by guiding the class in the formulation of a total church follow-up program using the concepts in this manual.

By developing a discipleship team trained for both individual attention and congregational attention, the church can lead new converts into consistent Christian growth.

Chapter 1

Dropouts or Disciples?

Objective of the Lesson

The best reason for putting in place a valid discipleship ministry in the local church is to stop the loss of converts. The church that launches an aggressive evangelism outreach to the community loses the fruit of that effort if it does not follow-up those who make a commitment to Jesus. The Body of Christ is the divinely ordained agency for the spiritual formation and growth of each new believer. The neglect of converts so widely practiced in modern evangelical churches stands in stark contrast to the churches of the first century. The book of Acts shows all converts to Christ being gathered in local churches where their nurture and maturation was a priority.

Group Activities

Activity One. Have the group consider the statement the author makes in the opening of the chapter:

> *Growth has been measured in terms of converts and that is not the best measure of success in evangelism. The most reliable measure of growth is the number of disciples added to the church. A disciple is a convert who is established in the Christian life and is functioning in the church.*

Is this just stacking up numbers or is this God's plan for the care of new converts?

Activity Two. Gather the statistics for your church over the past ten years comparing number of converts, baptisms and new members by confession of faith. Supply each member of the class with a set of blank graphs. Have them fill in the blanks as you provide the facts.

Lead the group by the use of these statistics through a self-study of the effectiveness or lack of effectiveness in the church's discipleship ministry.

* What kind of discipleship ministries are now being provided by the church?
* What do these graphs indicate as to the spiritual health of the church?
* What is happening to new converts?

On a blackboard or overhead projector make a list of the strengths and weaknesses the self-study indicates.

- The self-study should include a look at the church's total work force.

- What percentage of the believers are actively engaged in some form of service?

- How many workers would it take to bring the congregation to a full work force?

- How many members are actively engaged in evangelism?

- What is the church's present program for establishing new converts?

Questions for Discussion

1. What are the discernable signs in the life of the church of the neglect of discipleship?

2. Why is baptism important in the discipleship process?

3. How does church membership make a contribution to the maturation of a new Christian?

4. What aspects of ministry in your church would you consider essential to a newly saved person?

5. What kind of discipleship did you receive as a new believer?

6. How could your discipleship experience have been improved?

7. Name some of the losses the local church suffers as a result of the neglect of the care of converts?

8. Should lay people be involved in discipleship?

9. List the ministries of your church that could make a contribution to the process of nurturing converts.

10. What is the relationship between the lack of workers in the church and how the church deals with discipleship?

The Biblical Basis of Discipleship

Lead the class through an in-depth study of Hebrews 5:12-14. Read the entire fifth chapter in several versions to get in mind the context of the study passage.

- What indicated to the writer of Hebrews that these Christians were immature?

- What are the marks of a mature believer?

- How does poor discipleship adversely affect the growth of the church?

Chapter 2

What Is a Disciple?

Objective of the Lesson

The term *disciple* has a specialized meaning among all the words used to designate Christians. Exploring the synonyms for *disciple* found in the Gospels and the book of Acts helps to fill out the meaning of this term. Discipleship is a biblical idea. The principles of discipleship have often been used successfully in the secular world. In the days of Christ both Jews and Greeks used the discipleship method for training young people. Jesus enriched the concept of discipleship beyond that of the secular world. Christian discipleship is more than a learning process. It is an ongoing spiritual experience necessary to enjoying the full blessings of the gospel. This lesson is asking the question, "What is a disciple according to Christ's teachings?"

Group Activities

Activity One. Ask the group to study the five syno-

nyms of *disciple* found in this chapter and develop
from their considerations a definition of the word
disciple. Dictionaries and lexicons would be a good
resource for this activity.

Activity Two. Using the six issues of Christian discipleship found in John's Gospel, ask the group to
show how these issues are still relevant to modern
converts to Christ.

Questions for Discussion

1. What is the difference between being a convert and a disciple?

2. If Christ is the supreme Master-Teacher, does
   the convert need any other teacher? Support
   your answer with Scripture.

3. How important is the relationship of teacher
   to pupil in a good discipleship experience?

4. Does the discipleship process require the con-
   frontation of the convert with the biblical conditions for following Jesus? Name some of
   those conditions.

5. What is the true test of a real convert?

6. Why is discipline so essential for converts
   coming from today's culture?

7. How could the neglect of follow-up by local
   churches hinder world evangelism?

8. How does total devotion to Christ contribute
   to the establishment of a new convert?

Biblical Basis of Discipleship

- With the help of an analytical concordance find all the passages using the word *disciple* in the Gospel of John.

- Write a definition of the word *disciple* from what you have learned from these passages.

- Read the context of the following verses: John 8:31-32; 13:34-35; 15:7-8.

- What did Christ teach as to the central issue of discipleship?

- How did Jesus make disciples during His ministry?

Biblical Models of Discipleship

Objective of the Lesson

How to disciple is best learned by observing those who have been successful at it. The New Testament presents the earthly ministry of Christ as the first example of discipling. The four Gospels carefully record the method of the Master-Discipler as He day by day equipped His followers to carry out their mission for Him. The Acts of the Apostles and the Epistles offer many sketches of early Christians at work discipling new believers. The techniques demonstrated by these examples still work. Discipleship as displayed in the New Testament is a divine plan. These models teach us about one-on-one discipleship and congregational discipleship. Church life in the first century took in the care, maturation and nurture of those accepting Christ through their aggressive evangelism. Growth is the inevitable result of the marriage of evangelism and discipleship in the practice of any local church.

Group Activities

Activity One. Let the group compile a list of the personal traits of Barnabas, Ananias and Timothy that would make them good candidates for discipling new Christians. Discuss how temperament relates to nurturing new professors of Christ. From this discussion construct a temperament profile of the ideal discipler.

Activity Two. Read Colossians 1 in at least three modern versions and from this study write a goal for local church discipleship ministry.

Questions for Discussion

1. What evidence do you find that these early disciplers kept relating the convert to the church?

2. What did you learn from the example of Barnabas as to how to help new converts? Why might the church be suspicious about this?

3. What are the spiritual characteristics of the models in this chapter?

4. In what ways did Paul reproduce his life in Timothy as a result of their discipleship relationship?

5. How important is doctrine in discipling? Why?

6. Which models in this chapter show the signifi-
   cance of prayer and personal devotions in the
   discipleship process?

7. Is the guidance of the Holy Spirit essential to
   good discipling? Illustrate from the models.

8. How does the apostle John measure the spiritual age of the Christian? How is this helpful
   in the care of new converts?

Guide the class through a discussion of the six
examples of discipleship in this lesson. Help them
to see the personal and spiritual qualities which
made those disciples effective. This lesson gives
insight as to the methods used by these men to establish new believers. With the help of the class
compile as complete a list as possible of these
methods. Write them on the blackboard as they
are suggested. What application do they have to
the current needs of the church?

Follow the discussion of the men and the methods used in the early church with a consideration
of the theological issues of discipleship. These
may be drawn from First John 2:12-14 and Colossians 1:24-2:5. What principles of discipleship can
you find in the Great Commission?

More Questions for Discussion

1. What personal qualities did Barnabas have
   which fitted him for follow-up ministry?

2. In these examples of discipleship procedure
   what was the role of the total congregation?

3. Why is patience necessary for those who take up the ministry of discipling new converts?

4. What are the direct and the indirect results of the disciple's good example of the Christian life?

5. How much time do you suppose Barnabas devoted to discipling Saul of Tarsus?

6. What added dimensions to discipleship methods can be found in the example of Ananias?

7. How important is prayer and personal devotions to the disciples? Which scriptural model illustrates this truth?

8. What did Timothy expect of those he disciples?

9. How important is doctrine in the follow-up ministry?

10. Explain the importance of admonition in promoting the growth of a new believer.

Biblical Basis of Discipleship

Exposition of First John 2:12-14:

While most of the Scripture passages in this chapter show the disciplers at work, the passage from First John deals with the theology of discipleship. Prepare a visual display of the three age levels John mentions and the qualities which identify each of them. Trace the progression of growth through the three levels. How would a good understanding of this passage help to formulate a solid discipleship program? Compare John's approach to discipleship with that of Paul. What other New Testament passages describe the Christian life in terms of age levels? How do these passages infer the necessity for growth?

Helpful Resources

Bruce, F. F. *The Book of Acts*, The New International Commentary of the New Testament. (Grand Rapids, MI: William B. Eerdmans, 1971 edition).

Chapter 3

Talking with God

Your body cannot live without food. Neither can it live without air to breathe. Prayer is the breathing of your new life in Christ. Jesus said that believers ought to pray about everything so they will not become discouraged.

Praying is talking with God. It is necessary to be near to God in order to talk with Him. You cannot talk with someone who is far away and cannot hear you. When Christ saved you He brought you near to God. He opened heaven so you could talk with God the Father directly. You are invited to draw near to God (James 4:8).

The most enjoyable talks with God are the talks you have alone with Him, when no one else is with you. What should you talk with God about?

First of all, praise and thank Him for what He has done for you. Then tell God about your faults, weaknesses and sins, and ask the Lord to help you to be strong. Tell Him all your troubles and ask Him to guide you in your actions.

When you are worried and burdened about your loved ones and friends who have needs, tell God about them as you pray. Pray especially for those who need Christ. The heavenly Father is your Friend now, and He will be happy to listen to everything that is in your heart.

When it is possible, pray with other believers. Pray every day with those in your home. Gather your family together and let each one who believes pray. When other Christians visit your home, have prayer together before they leave. Meet often with other Christians for prayer.

Take time to pray. Christians learn to pray by praying.

Memorize Mark 11:24:

> *Therefore I tell you, whatever you ask for in prayer, believe that you have received it, and it will be yours.*

Answer these questions from the Bible:

1. Who gives you the right to pray to God? Whose name should you use? John 14:13-14; 16:23-24

   _____

   _____

   _____

   _____

2. To what kind of people does God give the privilege of prayer? 1 John 3:22; James 5:16

_____

_____

_____

3. What will happen if you pray and still have a desire to sin in your heart? Psalm 66:18

_____

_____

_____

_____

4. What does Matthew 21:22 tell you God expects from you if He is to answer your prayer?

_____

_____

_____

5. How do you know God will answer your prayer if you can't see how it will happen? Jeremiah 33:3; 1 John 5:14-15

_____

_____

_____

_____

6. How will praying keep you from worry? Philippians 4:6-7

_____

_____

_____

7. Who is your Helper when you pray? How
   does He help you? Romans 8:26

   _____

   _____

   _____

8. What is the key to our confidence in ap-
   proaching God? What is the result? 1 John
   5:14-15

   _____

   _____

   _____

9. What does God promise to those who pray
   together? Matthew 18:19-20

   _____

   _____

   _____

Chapter 4

A New Person

When you became a Christian you began a whole new life. A person living in sin is dead toward God. When one receives Christ he or she is truly made alive.

Bad habits, sinful pleasures, unclean thoughts and desires must be put away from the Christian. Paul says, "Therefore, if anyone is in Christ, he is a new creation; the old has gone, the new has come!" (2 Corinthians 5:17).

Ask the Holy Spirit to show you those things in your life belonging to the old life which must go. Give them up right away, and the Lord will make you strong.

Your mind now belongs to the Lord. Ask Him to make your thoughts clean. Be careful to fill your mind with good thoughts. Read only those things that will help you keep a clean mind.

The Bible teaches that a Christian's body is the temple of the Holy Spirit—a holy place where God's Spirit lives. Any habit that harms the body, then, is sinful. Keep your body clean and pure. Use your body for the Lord.

Satan will tempt you. He will use even your friends and loved ones. You are now a child of God. Make up your mind that you will not walk into Satan's trap.

Use wisdom in the way you spend your leisure time. Choose friends who will strengthen you spiritually. Decide that you will forsake the ways and thoughts of the old life in favor of the ways and the thoughts of the new life in Christ.

Beginning your new life with definite separation from the world, the flesh and the devil will bring you inner peace and give credibility to your testimony.

Memorize Second Corinthians 5:17:

Therefore, if anyone is in Christ, he is a new creation; the old has gone, the new has come!

Answer these questions from the Bible:

1. What are some specific sins that should not be in the lives of Christians? Galatians 5:19-21; Ephesians 4:25, 28, 31; 5:3

————————————————————

————————————————————

————————————————————

————————————————————

————————————————————

————————————————————

2. How should a Christian look at drinking?
   Proverbs 20:1

   _____

   _____

   _____

3. What does Second Corinthians 6:17-18 say
   about unclean things? How do Christians
   avoid them? Can you think of any unclean
   areas in your life you need to deal with?

   _____

   _____

   _____

4. What kinds of things should you think about
   to keep your mind clean? Philippians 4:8

   _____

   _____

   _____

5. What should you ask God to do about your
   thoughts? Psalm 139:23-24

   _____

   _____

   _____

6. How does Christ feel about iniquity or sin?
   Hebrews 1:9

   _____

   _____

   _____

   _____

7. What do Romans 6:1-2, 12, 14 say about sinning as a Christian?

_____

_____

_____

8. If you find out you have sinned, what should you do right away? What will God do?
   1 John 1:9

_____

_____

_____

Chapter 5

The Spirit-filled Life

The Holy Spirit comes to each believer to make him or her alive in Christ. The Spirit gives life and He sustains spiritual life daily. Christians are to have the Holy Spirit not only as Lifegiver, but they are to be filled with the Spirit.

The new believer may question, "How can I be filled with the Spirit?" To be filled with the Spirit is every believer's privilege. The Scriptures give the following conditions for being filled with the Holy Spirit. The first condition is consecrating oneself to God: "Therefore, I urge you, brothers, in view of God's mercy, to offer your bodies as living sacrifices, holy and pleasing to God—this is your spiritual act of worship" (Romans 12:1). The second condition is being willing to forsake all known sin and having a desire to be pure in heart (Acts 15:9). The third condition is having an attitude of ready obedience to the known will of God (Acts 5:32). The Scripture says, "Blessed are those who hunger and thirst for righteousness, for they will be filled" (Matthew 5:6). Jesus is teaching in this passage the value of spiritual desire. It is a necessary attitude for being filled with the Spirit.

When the believer understands, according to the Scriptures, the provision of the filling of the Spirit and has prepared his or her heart by meeting the above-mentioned conditions he is ready to pray. Jesus said, "If you then, though you are evil, know how to give good gifts to your children, how much more will your Father in heaven give the Holy Spirit to those who ask him!" (Luke 11:13). The believer comes to the Father in faith and simply asks that he or she be filled with the Spirit.

Jesus pictures the Spirit-filled life as a river of living water overflowing with blessing: "On the last and greatest day of the Feast, Jesus stood and said in a loud voice, 'If anyone is thirsty, let him come to me and drink. Whoever believes in me, as the Scripture has said, streams of living water will flow from within him'" (John 7:37-38). The fullness of the Spirit brings abundance, completeness, power and victory.

The Holy Spirit not only fills the heart but He sanctifies the whole spirit, soul and body of the believer. The word *sanctify* means to separate from sin and dedicate to God for His holy purpose. God's purpose, according to the Scriptures, is to make the believer Christlike. After the Christian is filled with the Spirit and wholly sanctified, the growth process is accelerated. Being filled with the Spirit is not an end in itself but the introduction of an ongoing growth and development of holy living. Maturity comes by a process of growth in the grace and the knowledge of the Lord Jesus Christ. It is futile to seek such growth apart from total consecration and the filling of the Holy Spirit.

The believer is not able to overcome weakness and sin in his or her own strength. The life of victory is assured by Christ living in the believer. Victorious living is made possible through the Holy Spirit, Christ's personal representative to each individual Christian. It is by the Holy Spirit that Christ lives in you.

Memorize Ephesians 5:18:

Do not get drunk on wine, which leads to debauchery. Instead, be filled with the Spirit.

Answer these questions from the Bible:

1. Who is the Holy Spirit? John 14:26; 16:13-14

_____

_____

_____

_____

2. What is the first ministry of the Holy Spirit? John 16:8

_____

_____

_____

_____

3. What is the Holy Spirit's work in the new
   birth? John 3:5; Titus 3:5

   _____

   _____

   _____

4. Who sanctifies the believer? What does it
   mean to be santified? 1 Peter 1:2

   _____

   _____

   _____

5. How does the Holy Spirit give power to the
   Christian? Ephesians 3:16-17

   _____

   _____

   _____

6. In what ways is your life changed by the
   Holy Spirit when you become a Christian?
   Romans 8:3-6

   _____

   _____

   _____

Chapter 6

Overcoming Temptation

It is only after becoming a Christian that you understand what temptation really is. After you have passed from the darkness of spiritual death to the light of eternal life in Christ you have virtually changed masters. Before salvation you served the devil; after salvation you serve Christ. The devil does not abandon his prey easily. He makes every subtle effort to turn the believer away from following Christ. The devil will deliberately try to entice the Christian to sin. Even the Lord Jesus Christ was tempted by the devil during His earthly life.

All Christians experience temptation in many forms. Sometimes the devil uses another person to tempt you or he may place an evil thought in your mind. Books, pictures, television, radio or any form of media may suggest wickedness—and even seek to make that wickedness look desirable.

God understands your battles with temptation and He has provided in His grace all the help you need to overcome temptation. Peter says that the devil goes about like a roaring lion. He does this to frighten the Christian and to make him or her feel helpless in the face of temptation. But the Word of God teaches that "the one who is in you is greater than the one who is in the world" (1 John 4:4). This means simply that Christ living in you is much stronger than the devil who is in the world.

Ask the Lord for His help and wisdom in overcoming temptation. Use the method Jesus used when He was tempted by the devil in the wilderness—He countered every suggestion of the devil with a Scripture passage. A good knowledge of the Bible will equip you to meet temptation.

Twice in the New Testament Christians are told to resist the devil.

"Resist him, standing firm in the faith" (1 Peter 5:9).

"Resist the devil, and he will flee from you" (James 4:7).

To resist the devil you must use your will. When you realize that the devil is trying to tempt you, immediately determine in your will to walk in God's way and not give in to the devil. By making that choice you will become stronger and will be able to overcome the temptation.

The crisis of temptation calls for the exercise of faith. The struggle with the tempter makes Christians aware of their many weaknesses and sends them to Christ for divine help. Paul called this spiritual action putting on the whole armor of God. As a soldier going into battle covers his vulnerable body with a metal armor, so the children of God in their battle with temptation need the covering of God's armor. At the cross Jesus won over the devil and crushed his power. This same victorious Christ will stand by your side in the hour of temptation and give you His strength. Revelation 12:11 says that the believers overcame Satan by the blood of the Lamb. Trust in the power of the blood and the devil will flee.

Memorize First Corinthians 10:13:

No temptation has seized you except what is common to man. And God is faithful; he will not let you be tempted beyond what you can bear. But when you are tempted, he will also provide a way out so that you can stand up under it.

Answer these questions from the Bible:

1. How does God help the believer when he or she is tempted to sin? 1 Corinthians 10:13

_____

_____

_____

_____

2. What areas of your life will the enemy use to tempt you? 1 John 2:16

_____

_____

_____

3. At what point can temptation become sin? James 1:13-15

_____

_____

_____

4. Make a list of the strategies of the devil to tempt the Christian. 2 Corinthians 4:3-4; 1 Peter 5:8-9

_____

_____

_____

5. Why should the believer understand the possible ways the devil may use to tempt him or her? 2 Corinthians 2:10-11

_____

_____

_____

6. What are the weapons of the Christian for this spiritual war with the devil? 2 Corinthians 10:3-6; Ephesians 6:10-18

_____

_____

_____

Chapter 7

Facing Up to Persecution

Life in Christ is realistic. Christ lived in our real world, so He is a sufficient Savior for all people. The Christian life works because it faces the tensions of living in an alien world. Unsaved people are not friends of God's goodness and righteousness. They do not understand people who regulate their lives by the will of God. New Christians should be aware of the pressure that may come upon them as a result of their stand for Christ. The Scriptures call this persecution.

Christ prepared His disciples for this reality:

> *Blessed are those who are persecuted because of righteousness, for theirs is the kingdom of heaven.*
>
> *Blessed are you when people insult you, persecute you and falsely say all kinds of evil against you because of me. Rejoice and be glad, because great is your reward in heaven, for in the same way they persecuted the prophets who were before you.* (Matthew 5:10-12)

Jesus Christ did not advocate a fatalistic accep-
tance of the pressures and even sufferings which
come to His people as a result of persecution. The
Sermon on the Mount lays down a basic spiritual
principle for dealing with persecution. Every
Christian needs to understand that principle.
Christ says that believers are persecuted because
of their identification with Him. He also teaches
in this passage that a proper reaction to persecution has its rewards both in this life and in the life
to come.

The biggest battle a new believer faces is reacting
wrongly to persecution from loved ones and friends.
This persecution may take more than one form.
Sometimes it is ridicule, or it may be disgust or even
hate. How should a Christian act when treated this
way by family members and associates? Jesus said
to bless those who misuse you. Do not retaliate. The
spirit of Christ is one of meekness and He calls His
disciples to react in the same spirit.

First Peter 4:12-16 says,

> *Dear friends, do not be surprised at the pain-*
> *ful trial you are suffering, as though something*
> *strange were happening to you. But rejoice that*
> *you participate in the sufferings of Christ, so*
> *that you may be overjoyed when his glory is re-*
> *vealed. If you are insulted because of the name of*
> *Christ, you are blessed, for the Spirit of glory*
> *and of God rests on you. If you suffer, it should*
> *not be as a murderer or thief or any other kind of*
> *criminal, or even as a meddler. However, if you*

suffer as a Christian, do not be ashamed, but praise God that you bear that name.

It is a privilege to suffer for Christ. Suffering resulting from the believer's own mistakes and inconsistent living can only be changed by repentance. But suffering resulting from the believer's choice to do God's will wholeheartedly is attended with deep inner peace and blessing. The Holy Spirit enables the yielded believer to respond to suffering with praise rather than self-pity. In the providential working of God's Spirit, often the gracious spirit of the sufferer will ultimately win the persecutor to Christ. The Christian ought not to look for trouble, but when it comes he should realize the abundance of grace to help bear it. The Christlike practice of forgiving those who misuse you makes your Christian witness credible.

Memorize Second Timothy 2:12:

If we endure, we will also reign with him. If we disown him, he will also disown us.

Answer these questions from the Bible:

1. Why does God permit believers to suffer for their faith? Romans 8:17; Philippians 3:10; Colossians 1:24

_____

_____

_____

2. What are the rewards of suffering for Christ? Romans 8:18; 2 Timothy 2:12

_____
_____
_____
_____

3. What comfort is offered to the Christian in times of persecution and suffering? 2 Timothy 4:16-18; John 16:33

_____
_____
_____
_____
_____

4. What should Christians do while they are suffering? 1 Peter 4:19

_____
_____
_____
_____

5. In what ways can suffering help to mature the believer? Romans 5:3-5

_____
_____
_____

6. What does suffering enable the child of God to do? How? 2 Corinthians 1:3-7

_____
_____
_____

Chapter 8

The Lord for the Body

The Lord Jesus Christ is a complete Savior. He purchased with His precious blood a redemption that includes the sinner's every need. It overcomes the results of sin and assures eternal life. The body of the Christian is included in redemption. Biblical salvation not only brings peace and spiritual blessing to the inner person, it includes the outer person as well. Salvation is for the whole person: spirit, soul and body.

The body is the temple of the Holy Spirit (1 Corinthians 6:19). The body is a member of Christ and therefore should be treated with reverence. The body is sanctified by Christ (1 Thessalonians 5:23). The body will be resurrected from the dead (1 Corinthians 15:20-23).

Health and healing are among the provisions of Christ for the Christian's body. Paul said, "The body is not meant for sexual immorality, but for the Lord, and the Lord for the body" (1 Corinthians 6:13). A wonderful new relationship is offered every Christian in this verse. As you present your body to Christ you may trust Christ for your bodily needs. The Lord Jesus Christ is Healer as well as Savior and Sanctifier.

The joy of the Christian life promotes good physical and mental health. But when the pressures of life bring illness on a child of God he or she may go to the Lord for healing. James instructs the Christian as to the procedure for asking healing of the Lord:

> *Is any one of you in trouble? He should pray. Is anyone happy? Let him sing songs of praise. Is any one of you sick? He should call the elders of the church to pray over him and anoint him with oil in the name of the Lord. And the prayer offered in faith will make the sick person well; the Lord will raise him up. If he has sinned, he will be forgiven. Therefore confess your sins to each other and pray for each other so that you may be healed. The prayer of a righteous man is powerful and effective.* (James 5:13-16)

Memorize First Corinthians 6:13:

> *"Food for the stomach and the stomach for food"—but God will destroy them both. The body is not meant for sexual immorality, but for the Lord, and the Lord for the body.*

Answer these questions from the Bible:

1. What is the basic cause of sickness in the human family? John 5:5-14

_____
_____
_____
_____

2. What specific promises can be found in these passages? Exodus 15:26; Psalm 103:1-3

_____
_____
_____
_____

3. What do these verses say about healing today? Luke 9:1; Mark 16:18; James 5:13-16

_____
_____
_____
_____

4. What is the role of the Holy Spirit in physical healing? Romans 8:11

_____
_____
_____
_____

5. What did Christ do to provide healing for
   His children? Isaiah 53:5; Matthew 8:17

   _____

   _____

   _____

   _____

6. What is the place of prayer in the ministry
   of healing? Acts 4:29-30; James 5:13-16

   _____

   _____

   _____

   _____

Chapter 9

Witnessing for Christ

The personal witness of believers is God's method for reaching other people. Witnessing is confessing that Jesus Christ is your Savior, expressing your personal faith in Him.

Everyone should hear the good news of the gospel. The best way for others to hear about Christ is for you to tell them. Paul tells us that just as we believe in our heart we must also confess with our mouth that we have a personal faith in Christ as our Savior:

> *That if you confess with your mouth, "Jesus is Lord," and believe in your heart that God raised him from the dead, you will be saved. For it is with your heart that you believe and are justified, and it is with your mouth that you confess and are saved.* (Romans 10:9-10)

Telling others is an important part of starting

your life with Christ and of living this new life from day to day. Peter said believers must always be ready to tell those who ask the reason for their trust in Christ: "But in your hearts set apart Christ as Lord. Always be prepared to give an answer to everyone who asks you to give the reason for the hope that you have" (1 Peter 3:15).

Jesus wants to use you in winning others to Himself. Start telling your family and friends today about the new peace you have in Christ. Pray about bringing others to Jesus. Ask the Holy Spirit to give you the power to speak the right words at the right time. He will guide you to people hungry for the gospel.

Every time you have opportunity to speak for Christ, do it. Faithfulness in witnessing strengthens your faith and gives great joy. As you read your Bible, mark the verses that will help you explain the plan of salvation to others. Get a supply of gospel tracts and be prepared to use them as tools in expressing your faith.

Memorize Proverbs 11:30:

"The fruit of the righteous is a tree of life, and he who wins souls is wise."

Answer these questions from the Bible:

1. What does the Bible say about a person who wins souls and brings people to God? Proverbs 11:30

_____
_____
_____
_____

2. What condition must we meet and how are we made "fishers of men"? Matthew 4:18-19

_____
_____
_____
_____

3. To what is the Christian asked to bear witness? Acts 2:32

_____
_____
_____

4. What did Andrew and Philip do after they found Christ as their Savior? John 1:40-46

_____
_____
_____
_____

5. How can you show God to others? Matthew 5:16

_____
_____
_____
_____

6. What is the reward in Daniel 12:3 for?

_____

_____

_____

_____

7. Jesus said that bringing others to Him is like harvesting a crop. When is the harvest ready? How can you help bring in the harvest? John 4:35

_____

_____

_____

_____

8. What is worth more than your soul? Mark 8:36-37

_____

_____

_____

9. What are we instructed to do? How can you carry this out? 1 Peter 3:15

_____

_____

_____

10. Think about Mark 16:15 and Luke 14:23. Where does Jesus ask you to go with the gospel? What sacrifices might this require?

_____

_____

_____

Chapter 10

Giving to God

God's Word says, "It is more blessed to give than to receive" (Acts 20:35). Sin makes one selfish. God gives the Christian a new mind so that he or she wants to give. Believers willingly give their life, strength, time, money and whatever they own to the Lord.

God owns everything, and you are just using what really belongs to Him. God is happy to give you whatever you need. Because of all that Christ has done for you, it should be easy for you to give back to Him whatever He may ask.

The Bible teaches the believer to tithe. This means he or she should give to God at least ten percent of everything earned (Malachi 3:10).

If every Christian would obey God by tithing, there would always be enough money for God's work. Start now to tithe. Obedience to God will bring rich blessings from the Lord.

The believer's love for God motivates him to give to God. That which is given above the tithe is a love offering to God.

You must manage your money well in order to give as you should. Some Christians rob themselves of the joy of giving because they have made poor commitments of their money, so they have nothing to give God.

Money is a necessary means of exchange in our modern world and Scripture recognizes this reality. The Bible also recognizes the menace that money can be in the life of a believer. The sin of covetousness is deadly, twisting the personality so that the person in its grip lives to accumulate money.

The Word of God teaches the believer how to use his or her money for the glory of God. Money management for the Christian is not just for the purpose of giving but because it represents a lifestyle compatible with divine standards.

Memorize Second Corinthians 9:7:

> *Each man should give what he has decided in his heart to give, not reluctantly or under compulsion, for God loves a cheerful giver.*

Answer these questions from the Bible:

1. What should be your motives for giving? 2 Corinthians 9:7

_____

_____

_____

_____

2. What does God promise if you obediently tithe? Malachi 3:10

_____

_____

_____

3. God's Word says giving is like planting seeds because later you get back more than you planted. What will happen if you don't give? 2 Corinthians 9:6

_____

_____

4. On what day of the week should Christians bring their gifts for God to church? 1 Corinthians 16:2

_____

_____

5. Read Matthew 6:19-21. What are your "treasures"? How do you know whether or not they're the right kind, stored in the right place?

_____

_____

6. Read the story in Mark 12:41-44. Why do you think Jesus was so pleased with what this woman did?

_____

_____

_____

7. Read Second Corinthians 8:9. What kind of example did Jesus give us by what He did for us?

_____

_____

_____

8. What does Psalm 41:1-3 say about the poor? What benefits are involved?

_____

_____

_____

9. What does Romans 10:14-15 ask us to do for people who are not saved?

_____

_____

_____

Chapter 11

A Church Home

The Lord Jesus Christ established His church as the spiritual home of believers. His church includes all true believers—of the past and of the present. When you believed on Christ as your Savior, you were baptized by the Spirit into Christ's body, the Church.

The Church is both visible and invisible—part of the whole Church being scattered throughout the world and part having already gone to be with the Lord in heaven. Christians must have more than a spiritual connection with the Church; they must identify themselves with the visible Church by becoming members of it.

A Christian needs fellowship with other believers. That fellowship may be found in a Bible-believing church which provides preaching, teaching and prayer. Meeting together with other Christians will help to strengthen your faith in the Lord Jesus Christ.

Jesus authorized the church to administer two

ordinances for the spiritual good of His people—
water baptism and the communion meal. You
need the church because only there can you par-
take of these ordinances commanded by Christ.

Water baptism pictures the steps of salvation.
As the repentant believer is immersed in the
water, it symbolizes his or her identification
with Christ in His death and burial. The baptis-
mal candidate is saying to the world, "I stand
with Christ and I believe His blood washes my
sins away." As the believer is raised from the
water the resurrection is in view. He or she is
now raised to walk in newness of life through
the power of the indwelling Christ (Romans 6:3-
4).

Christ instituted communion as a reminder of
His death for us and as a reminder that He is coming again. Communion is a term of fellowship
when believers break bread (symbolizing Christ's
body) together and drink the cup (symbolizing
Christ's blood), remembering they have been
made one by the death and resurrection of Christ.

Since being baptized and becoming a member
of the church is so important, ask your counselor
or the pastor about enrolling in the membership
class in order to prepare yourself for this step of
spiritual progress.

Memorize Matthew 18:20:

> *For where two or three come together in my
> name, there am I with them.*

Answer these questions from the Bible:

1. Who started the church? Matthew 16:16-18

_____

_____

_____

_____

2. Who is the leader or the "head" of the church? Ephesians 1:20-23

_____

_____

_____

_____

3. What requirement for church membership is given in this verse? Acts 2:47

_____

_____

_____

_____

4. Why is it important to attend church regularly? Hebrews 10:25

_____

_____

_____

_____

5. What spiritual steps come before water baptism? Acts 2:38; Mark 16:16

_____

_____

_____

_____

6. What is the purpose of communion?
   1 Corinthians 11:23-26

   _____

   _____

   _____

   _____

7. What happens when Christians meet in
   Christ's name? Matthew 18:20

   _____

   _____

   _____

   _____

Chapter 12

The Blessed Hope

The night before Jesus went to the cross He met in an upper room with His disciples. He told them a wonderful secret. Though God's plan of salvation required that Christ die on the cross, be buried, be raised from the dead and then return to the Father in heaven, there was still another step in this great plan: Jesus promised His disciples He would personally come back again (John 14:3). Christ's second coming will occur in two phases. The first phase of this great event will be to gather all true believers to Himself.

Paul tells exactly how this will take place:

> *Brothers, we do not want you to be ignorant about those who fall asleep, or to grieve like the rest of men, who have no hope. We believe that Jesus died and rose again and so we believe that God will bring with Jesus those who have fallen asleep in him. According to the Lord's own*

word, we tell you that we who are still alive,
who are left till the coming of the Lord, will cer-
tainly not precede those who have fallen asleep.
For the Lord himself will come down from
heaven, with a loud command, with the voice of
the archangel and with the trumpet call of God,
and the dead in Christ will rise first. After that,
we who are still alive and are left will be caught
up together with them in the clouds to meet the
Lord in the air. And so we will be with the Lord
forever. Therefore encourage each other with
these words. (1 Thessalonians 4:13-18)

For Christians who are alive when Jesus comes,
an instantaneous change will occur in their bodies.
The perishable mortal body will changed to a
body like Christ's beyond the reach of death. At
the time of Christ's return, the body of the dead
believer will be resurrected and shall be caught up
to meet Christ in the air. Paul spoke of Christ's
coming for His own as the "blessed hope." The
coming of Christ for His church is imminent. Jesus taught His disciples to live in constant readi-
ness for the Lord's return.

The second coming of Christ is not only the believer's personal hope and answer to the future; it is
also his or her key to understanding the world in
which he or she lives. Christ gave insight into the
signs at the end of the age and of His second coming. Jesus taught that wickedness would continue to
worsen in the world system and that demonic activity would be intensified. The apostle Paul described

the last days as dangerous because of social unrest, violence and evil. Political systems will be devastated. Finally, in the dark hours of the tribulation (a period of judgment Christ has designed to deal with the nations of the world), Satan will bring forth his masterpiece, a world ruler called the antichrist. This diabolic leader will bring the wickedness of the nations to its highest level.

Then the Lord Jesus will return to the earth with His saints to establish His kingdom. Then Satan will be bound and the righteous government of Christ will prevail among all the nations of the world. The true believers will reign with Christ during the thousand years His kingdom will be on earth. At the end of the 1,000-year reign the earth will be judged with fire. Christ will then judge the wicked from His great white throne. After these events the new heavens and the new earth will begin. The saints will dwell in the city of God and enjoy the blessings of Christ's everlasting kingdom.

Memorize John 14:3:

> And if I go and prepare a place for you, I will come back and take you to be with me that you also may be where I am.

Answer these questions from the Bible:

1. What present world conditions can you find described by Jesus in Matthew chapter 24?

_____
_____
_____
_____

2. Why did Paul refer to the second coming of Christ as "the blessed hope"? Titus 2:11-14

_____
_____
_____
_____

3. Where will Christ meet His people at the second coming? 1 Thessalonians 4:16-17

_____
_____
_____

4. What will take place in the believer when he or she is caught up to meet the Lord? 1 Thessalonians 4:17; 1 Corinthians 15:50-54; Philippians 3:20-21

_____
_____
_____
_____

5. How may the believer prepare for the Lord's coming? 1 John 3:1-3; 1 Peter 4:7-10; 2 Peter 3:11, 14

_____
_____
_____
_____

6. What is the responsibility of the Church until Christ returns? Matthew 28:19-20; Acts 1:8

_____

_____

_____

7. In the last days before Christ's coming what kinds of false reli-gions will appear? 1 Timothy 4:1-5

_____

_____

_____

8. How many resurrections do you find in the following Scripture? 1 Corinthians 15:20-24; Revelation 20:4-6

_____

_____

_____

9. By what will all people be judged? Revelation 20:11-15

_____

_____

_____

_____

10. List the characteristics of Christ's kingdom on earth after His return. Matthew 25:34; Isaiah 35; Zechariah 14:4-11; Isaiah 2:1-5; Revelation 19:11-16; 20:1-4

_____

_____

_____